The Twin Pillars of Healing

In this guide, Stephen Sinatra, M.D., reveals how an explosive combination of the nutrients coenzyme Q10 and L-carnitine—the twin pillars of healing—can have an exciting, positive impact on the cardiovascular system. He proves that this powerful combination not only supports the metabolism of fats, carbohydrates, and proteins but also provides and supports the production of ATP, the energy of life.

About the Authors

Stephen T. Sinatra, M.D., F.A.C.C., is a board-certified cardiologist, a certified bioenergetic psychotherapist, a fellow of the American College of Cardiology, Director of Medical Education at the Manchester Memorial Hospital, and an Assistant Clinical Professor of Medicine at the University of Connecticut School of Medicine. For over two decades, Dr. Sinatra has helped patients prevent and reverse heart disease utilizing conventional medical treatments as well as complementary nutritional and psychological therapies at his New England Heart Center in Manchester, Connecticut.

The author of *Heartbreak and Heart Disease*, the Good Health Guide *Coenzyme Q10 and the Heart*, and other best-selling books, Dr. Sinatra also serves as editor for *HeartSense*, a monthly newsletter devoted to healing the heart.

Jan Sinatra, R.N., M.S.N., is in private practice and has been a cardiac care unit nurse and a cardiac rehabilitation specialist for ten years. She received her Bachelor of Arts at the University of Connecticut and her Master of Science in Nursing at Yale University. She also serves as the editorial assistant for *HeartSense* newsletter.

Acknowledgments

The authors wish to acknowledge the transcribing and technical assistance of Donna Chaput and Nijole Bushnell. In addition, the editorial and research support of Christian Allan, Ph.D., Ken Hassen, Hemmi Bhagavan, Ph.D., Stanley Jankowitz, Mel Rich, and Raj Chopra was very much appreciated.

L-Carnitine and the Heart

Stephen T. Sinatra, M.D., F.A.C.C
with Jan Sinatra, R.N., M.S.N.

KEATS PUBLISHING

LOS ANGELES

NTC/Contemporary Publishing Group

L-Carnitine and the Heart is intended solely for informational and educational purposes and not as medical advice. Please consult a medical or health professional if you have questions about your health.

L-CARNITINE AND THE HEART

Published by Keats Publishing
A division of NTC/Contemporary Publishing Group, Inc.
4255 West Touhy Avenue, Lincolnwood (Chicago), Illinois 60712, U.S.A.
Copyright © 1999 by Stephen T. Sinatra, M.D., F.A.C.C.
Printed and bound in the United States of America
International Standard Book Number: 0-658-01163-4

19 20 DIG/DIG 15 14 13

Contents

Introduction 7
  L-Carnitine and Coenzyme Q10:
    The "Twin Pillars of Healing" 7
  Helen's Story 7
Mighty Mitochondria: Energy Powerplants 10
  Take Care of Your Mitochondria and Delay Aging 12
  How Aging Affects the Mitochondria 12
  How to Protect Your Mitochondria 13
L-Carnitine: What, Where, When, and Why? 15
  L-Carnitine and the Diet 15
  Biosynthesis of L-Carnitine 17
  Biological Effects of L-Carnitine 18
  Pharmacokinetics and Bioavailability 21
  Why Carnitine Deficiency? 22
L-Carnitine and the Heart 24
Angina and Heart Attack 27
  Understanding Angina 27
  Traditional Treatment for Angina 29
  L-Carnitine and Angina 30
  Carnitine and Acute Myocardial Infarction 33
Congestive Heart Failure 35
Peripheral Vascular Disease, Arrhythmia,
  Lipid Disorders, and Adriamycin Toxicity 39
  Peripheral Vascular Disease 39
  Cardiac Arrhythmia 41
  Carnitine and Kidney Disease 44
  Carnitine: Triglycerides and Cholesterol 45
  Adriamycin Toxicity 46
  Summary of Cardiovascular Interactions 47
Carnitine and Coenzyme Q10: Antiaging
  Nutrients for Health and Longevity 47

L-Carnitine Fumarate.. 50
Hydrosoluble Coenzyme Q10............................... 52
Dosage Recommendations, Drug Interactions,
    and Adverse Reactions... 54
Other Interactions... 55
Adverse Drug Interactions 55
Summary 56
References.. 57

L-CARNITINE AND COENZYME Q10*:
THE "TWIN PILLARS OF HEALING"

One of the most important discoveries physicians and scientists have made in recent years is that many nutrients tend to work better together. This "synergy" of nutrients often provides results superior to that of any single nutrient. After all, the body's many complex systems rely on a variety of nutrients to function properly. Think of it this way: in math, one plus one equals two. But when you add the right nutrients together that can work synergistically, one plus one *could* equal five or even ten! You don't merely add up the benefits of each nutrient. Instead, an explosive combination of nutrients can have an exciting, positive impact on one's well-being and even life itself. Let me tell you about a case that literally transformed a bedridden heart patient into an active grandma.

HELEN'S STORY

Helen is an eighty-five-year-old woman with a history of heart attack at age sixty-two. She had her first coronary artery bypass surgery in 1979. Helen had six brothers and sisters, and all of them died of heart-related causes. She is the only one still alive in her family. Although she had coronary bypass surgery again in 1987 and multiple attempts at PTCA (percutaneous coronary artery angioplasty), she still had a fair quality of life using a combination of medical and complementary therapies. For years she took phytonutrient supports, and by April of 1998, she was

*Sigma-tau U.S. patent #4,599,232.

taking the equivalent of 600 mg a day of coenzyme Q10 (CoQ10) to support her cardiac function and boost her energy.

Then the bottom dropped out! Helen became exhausted and fell into despair. Her vital life force and her energy were completely sapped. In fact, it became a Herculean task just to get up from her bed and sit in her chair. After battling heart problems for more than twenty years, Helen finally resigned herself to the fact that she was going to give in to her long battle against chronic heart failure and vital exhaustion, and just die. When she arrived at my office that day, her breathing was labored, she had shortness of breath, her energy level was completely zero, and the look in her eyes told me that she needed a miracle.

Although coenzyme Q10 has been a literal lifesaver for many of my patients with heart disease, in Helen's case something else was needed to provide that extra "spark" to make her come alive again. She needed something even more powerful to battle the severity of her heart problems and the ravages of advancing age. So, when she came to see me in April of 1998, I added an amino acid called L-carnitine to her game plan that she took along with her CoQ10.

L-carnitine is a compound that is produced in the liver and kidneys. High concentrations can be found in skeletal muscle as well as heart muscle. Over the years, I have read lots of literature about its clinical efficacy in animals and humans, and I have prescribed it for many of my patients. Since L-carnitine has been shown in numerous investigations to demonstrate favorable effects on the cardiovascular system, and especially since it had helped my other patients, I decided to give it to Helen.

Just four weeks later, you would hardly have recognized Helen! The color in her cheeks was much pinker, she was breathing easier, and she was able to move around freely for the first time in weeks. Soon after, Helen was active and mobile, puttering around her house, and before you knew it she was zipping around a shopping mall and going to grocery stores. In fact, I even saw her pushing a cart full of groceries at our local supermarket. And as if that weren't enough, Helen was even able to significantly reduce her dependence on some of the prescription drugs I had prescribed for her, particularly nitroglycerin.

When it comes to cardiac disease, L-carnitine has become one of my "twin pillars" of healing and prevention. You will soon see that L-carnitine can rocket your heart and muscle energy to new heights. It does this by maximizing the amount of oxygen that your heart and skeletal muscle can extract from your blood, oxygen that is vital to producing the energy that keeps your heart beating. In fact, since free fatty acids (i.e., fats) are the major fuel for the heart to pump effectively, L-carnitine's crucial role is that it supports the oxidation of these fatty acids in the inner mitochondrial membrane. *Free fatty acids* is a biochemical term for fat. Fats are generally composed of a hydrocarbon chain and an organic acid. They are called free fatty acids because they are "free" to move around in the blood and within cells, compared to fats (and lipids) that are part of a membrane, and so are stationary. As we shall see, the critical movement of some "free" fatty acids into the mitochondria requires L-carnitine, and so free fatty acids are not really so free.

Research shows that the heart uses free fatty acids as its main energy source.[1] More energy can be obtained from the breakdown of fats than from a comparable amount of carbohydrate, sugar, or starch. You soon shall see that the combination of coenzyme Q10 and L-carnitine not only supports the metabolism of fats, carbohydrates, and proteins but also provides and supports the production of ATP, the energy of life. We shall say more about this later.

The synergistic combination of L-carnitine and CoQ10 has been a tremendous breakthrough in the treatment of heart disease. Because L-carnitine and CoQ10 both work in the inner mitochondrial membrane, the clinical uses of carnitine and CoQ10 complement one another. This synergism goes well beyond the concept of the biochemistry of energy. Clinically, both CoQ10 and L-carnitine will reduce arrhythmia, reduce the risk of heart failure, and relieve cramping in the lower extremities (claudication). This new one-two punch—coenzyme Q10 and L-carnitine—is not only remarkably effective in preserving heart health but also is effective in preserving brain health, triggering weight loss, offering protection in neurodegenerative diseases (particularly Alzheimer's), giving new hope for male infertility, slowing down aging, improving immunity, and even enhancing athletic performance.

You probably have never heard about this exciting combination of CoQ10 and L-carnitine, let alone read about it in any publication or on the Internet. This Good Health Guide will specifically discuss L-carnitine's positive impact on the cardiovascular system. For those of you interested in a thorough analysis of the power of coenzyme Q10, I refer you to my previous book, *The Coenzyme Q10 Phenomenon*. And now, let's go on to discuss the fundamentals of L-carnitine, one of two precious ingredients that make up the "twin pillars of healing" in cardiovascular disease. Our discussion begins with the vital importance of mitochondria.

MIGHTY MITOCHONDRIA: ENERGY POWERPLANTS

While studying for the antiaging boards many years ago, I was forced to consider exactly *how* people age, why we develop diseases, and even why some of us die prematurely. Of all the theories of aging, it was the *free radical theory* and its relationship to mitochondria that made the most health sense to me. So what exactly are mitochondria?

It was more than fifty years ago that mitochondria became the focus of much scrutiny. You may remember from high school biology that the mitochondria are the "powerhouse" part of the cell responsible for energy production. They are probably the most important *cellular organelle* because without them energy cells cease to function, and if too many of them stop working, you become much weaker.

Mitochondria actually have two sets of membranes: the smooth continuous outer coat and the inner membrane, which is arranged in folds called cristae. These tiny powerplants for biological energy production create more than 90 percent of the energy we need to support metabolism and growth and to sustain life.

Adenosine triphosphate (ATP) is produced in the mitochondria, which are inside all of our cells. This high-energy phosphate compound is necessary to fuel all cellular functions. Think of ATP as a high-octane fuel used for all the energetic transactions in your body. We may think we eat only to satisfy our hunger or our taste buds or as a social activity. But the truth is, we consume food to get the energy sources required to generate ATP, the body's major form of stored energy.

Inside the mitochondria, fatty acids (fats) are oxidized by oxygen. This process releases electrons that travel down the respiratory chain and, during this process, make ATP. The ATP is eventually transported to various parts of the cell to supply energy when needed. It is the generation of this energy that supplies the vital force so necessary for life. This whole process of energy formation and transfer is called *respiration*. The final products that are generated by fatty acid oxidation are water and carbon dioxide. We release carbon dioxide (and some water) when we exhale. Photosynthetic plants use these two simple molecules, along with the energy from the sun, to generate carbohydrates, which get eaten by animals and stored as fat. We ultimately eat the fat for our own energy, and the cycle of life between plants and animals continues.

During the respiration process, not all of the oxygen gets converted to water. Some oxygen, from 2 to 5 percent, does not get completely reduced and instead becomes a toxic molecule. This may be confusing to you, but let me explain. Although oxygen is necessary for aerobic life, the improper metabolism of oxygen has ominous consequences for your body. Numerous investigations suggest that oxidant by-products of normal metabolism, known as free radicals, are involved in the process not only of the degenerative diseases of the twentieth century but also of aging itself.

However, free radicals also play a key role in normal biological functions. Obviously, this seems to be a paradox. Research has shown that free radicals may play a fundamental role in supporting life processes such as mitochondrial respiration,[2] platelet activation,[3] and killer white blood cell activity.[4] Yet these unstable, highly reactive, and damaging molecular species have been found to cause extensive damage to lipid membranes, organelles like mitochondria, and even DNA itself. This paradox of free radical chemistry has generated enormous interest among health-care professionals, especially those interested in preventive and antiaging medicine.

When ATP is generated in mitochondria (the powerful furnaces that generate energy), reactive oxygen species (ROS), or free radicals, are formed inside the mitochondrial membrane. With continuous energy production taking place, free radicals can accumulate rapidly. This affects the health of the mitochondria themselves. So what can we do to help prevent this or even reverse this process?

TAKE CARE OF YOUR MITOCHONDRIA AND DELAY AGING

Do you ever give your houseplants natural fertilizers, then watch them bloom and reach for the sun? Well, your mitochondria need the same loving care to keep your body healthy and vibrant and to prolong your life. Recent research suggests that we can "fertilize" mitochondria with selected nutrients to delay the death of cells, which we now believe to be *the* main cause of premature aging, illness, and death. Since so many of us do not consume the correct balance of foods to supply all the nutrients we need, supplementation has now become a way of life.

Why is it that an eighty-five-year-old person can pole vault, while a fifty-year-old person can look and act like an eighty-year-old? It's no mystery. If mitochondria are healthy, then so are we. If these powerhouses are damaged in any way, we're in trouble. We can get any number of degenerative diseases, including heart disease, cancer, or Alzheimer's. Indeed, mitochondria are likely the key to how we age, why we get disease, and why some of us die prematurely.

HOW AGING AFFECTS THE MITOCHONDRIA

Aging in itself puts a considerable strain on mitochondria. Let me give you an example. When energy can't be delivered to the aging heart, which has the greatest concentration of mitochondria, congestive heart failure (CHF) may follow.

At least once a month I see a new patient, usually a woman in her seventies or eighties, who has a new onset of congestive heart failure. If I can't find the underlying cause of the problem—previous heart attack, chronic high blood pressure, leaky valve, or recent infection—then I immediately suspect that my patient's CHF is triggered by deteriorating mitochondria and insufficient levels of two key nutrients: coenzyme Q10 and L-carnitine.

When these conditions occur, the heart cells lack sufficient energy to pulsate properly. Over time, this affects the heart's ability to pump effectively. Most cells in your body contain about 500 to 2,000 mitochondria. That's a staggering number to imagine. But your heart muscle cells have the greatest concentration, perhaps as many as 5,000 in each cell (almost 50 percent of the total cell volume)! The heart is the most pulsatile of all our organs; tremendous energy is required to pump all your blood. And when that energy can't be delivered, congestive heart failure follows. As your mitochondria keep banging out all those chemical reactions, they're subjected to a lot of wear and tear. I believe this is why there are so many "unexplained" cases of heart failure. In fact, approximately 30 percent of new cases of congestive heart failure have no known cause. Someday research will probably show that mitochondrial, cellular, and metabolic dysfunctions are the culprits. For now, a clever cardiologist should always keep in mind the possibility of mitochondrial dysfunction in unexplained heart failure.

HOW TO PROTECT YOUR MITOCHONDRIA

To help neutralize free radical stress, nurture your mitochondria, and delay aging, I believe that your personal "damage control" should consist of *lifelong treatment* with these five supplements: coenzyme Q10, L-carnitine, alpha lipoic acid, and vitamins E and C. These nutrients are also exceptional for protecting our vascular membranes from atherosclerosis as well. Early atherosclerosis is premature aging.

CoQ10 and *L-carnitine* are essential for the production of ATP. CoQ10's role as an electron carrier in the mitochondrial electron transfer chain makes it the pivotal nutrient for the production of cellular energy. In biochemical terms, coenzyme Q10 supports every cell in the human body by keeping the electron transport chain functioning properly. It is this key bioenergetic property that makes coenzyme Q10 so unique.

L-carnitine functions like a freight train, transporting crucial fatty acids across the mitochondrial membrane to be burned as fuel. It is essential for the transfer of long-chain and short-chain fatty acids from the cytoplasm to the mitochondria, permitting beta-oxidation (the term given to fatty acid oxidation within the mitochondria) and producing energy in the form of ATP. This is why there is tremendous synergism between these two nutrients.

Figure 1 Beta-Oxidation Process

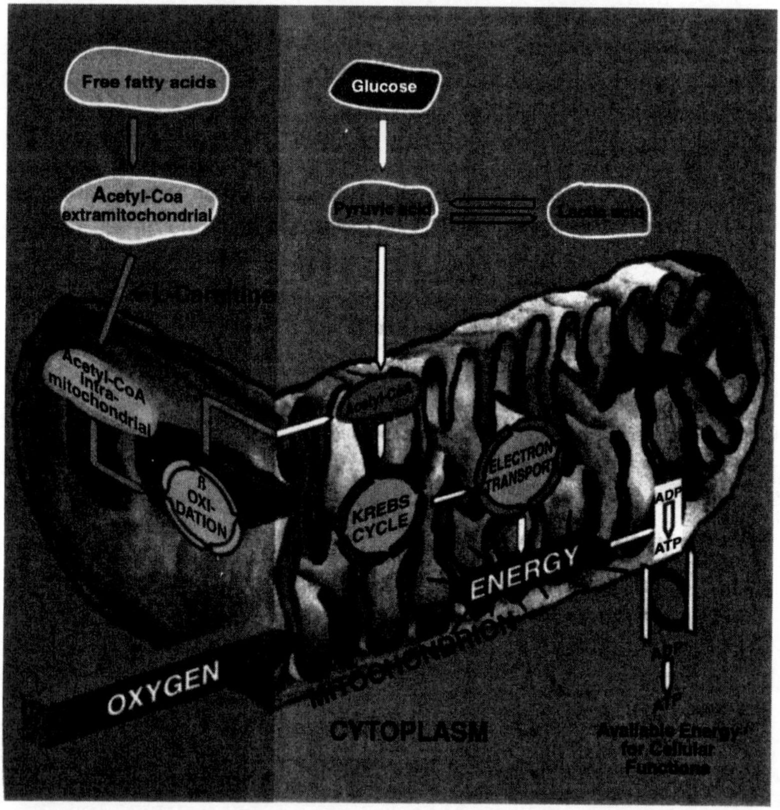

L-carnitine and CoQ10 are vital for life to exist. L-carnitine and coenzyme Q10 typically are not classified as vitamins, because they can be taken in the diet as well as formed in the body. However, as we age, the production of both coenzyme Q10 and carnitine may decrease, so nutritional support, in the form of greater food intakes that contain these nutrients and supplementation of them, may be crucial in maintaining optimal health. CoQ10 and carnitine combinations may offer protection against aging.

Alpha lipoic acid helps regenerate vitamins E and C once they've been oxidized. Its general function is to couple electron transfers with group transfers. One of the most important is in the conversion of pyruvate, which is derived from the breakdown of sugar, into acetyl-coenzyme A (Acetyl-CoA). Acetyl-CoA is the molecule in the mitochondria where energy production begins (see Figure 1). Acetyl-CoA is also formed by beta-oxidation of fatty acids. Alpha lipoic acid also crosses the blood-brain barrier and helps neutralize the effects of toxic metals, which can damage mitochondria.

Vitamin E helps prevent the oxidation of LDL (bad cholesterol). CoQ10 helps to recycle oxidized vitamin E back to its active form. Together they both protect blood vessels from oxidative stress.

Vitamin C has many functions. It is known to inhibit the oxidation of LDL and support the production of reduced glutathione, the common natural antioxidant that preserves blood vessels and strengthens the immune system.

A little mitochondrial repair and nurturing may delay the aging process and may even prevent diseases like cancer, heart disease, and Alzheimer's. Wouldn't you like to live a little healthier and perhaps even longer too? There's an old saying, "Add years to your life, and life to your years." Sounds good to me! So, let's discuss the history of L-carnitine, its biochemical structure, and how it works.

L-CARNITINE: WHAT, WHERE, WHEN, AND WHY?

Like coenzyme Q10, L-carnitine belongs to a group of vitamin-like nutrients. They are similar to vitamins in that they are not only obtained from the diet through food sources; they are also synthesized by the body. Since coenzyme Q10 and carnitine synthesis may diminish with aging, relative deficiencies may exist over time. This is why it may be important to get L-carnitine both in the diet and in supplemental form.

L-CARNITINE AND THE DIET

Carnitine is actually derived from two amino acids: lysine and methionine. Biosynthesis occurs in both human and other mammals in a series of metabolic reactions involving these amino acids, complemented with niacin, vitamin B[6], vitamin C, and iron. Although L-carnitine deficiency is an infrequent problem in a healthy, well-nourished population consuming adequate protein, many people appear to be somewhere on the continuum between mild deficiency and overt disease.[5] Consider, for example, the vegetarian population.

Like coenzyme Q10, sources of L-carnitine can be deficient in people who are pure vegetarians. In my practice of cardiology, I've examined many vegetarians with low coenzyme Q10 levels and, most likely, low carnitine levels as well. Remember, the word *carnitine* comes from "carnis," meaning flesh or meat. The greatest quantities of carnitine are found in mutton from older sheep, followed by lamb, beef, other red meat, and pork. Although carnitine is found in many foods, the quantities in plants are exceedingly small (see Table 1). Vegetarians, in a way, are "behind the eight ball." Not only do pure vegetarians fail to get enough carnitine in their diet, they may lack methionine and lysine as well.

Table 1   The Amount of L-Carnitine in Some Types of Foods

Meats	mm/gm
Sheep	12.90
Lamb	4.80
Beef	3.80
Pork	1.90
Poultry	.60
Other Foods	mm/gm
Pears	0.17
Rice	0.11
Asparagus	0.08
Margarine	0.08
Peas	0.07
Bread	0.05
Potatoes	0.00
Carrots	0.00

Note: Highest quantities of L-carnitine are found in mutton and lamb.

For example, beans are a rich source of protein containing lysine but generally are deficient in methionine, while rice contains plenty of methionine but lacks lysine. Both methionine and lysine are essential amino acids required for the biosynthesis of L-carnitine. Thus, in a vegetarian diet that relies upon lots of beans and rice, these two essential amino acids are lacking. The L-carnitine concentration in vegetables and fruits is approximately 90 percent less than that in meats, and in cereals it is less than 5 percent. When I encounter vegetarians in my practice, I insist that they consider not only vitamin B_{12} and CoQ10 supplementation, but L-carnitine as well.

There are documented cases of people following strict macrobiotic diets who develop weakness, weight loss, and severe nutritional deficiencies, which then may result in disease.[6] It also is well established that both children and adults consuming primarily vegetarian-type foods tend to have lower concentrations of carnitine in their plasma compared to those eating foods rich in animal sources.[7]

There also are many anecdotal cases where L-carnitine deficiency resulted from a vegetarian diet in the individual's infancy or childhood. Many of these patients show muscle weakness and a failure to thrive associated with *osteomalacia* (failure in bone development).[8] The biosynthesis of carnitine in rodents yielded four times more carnitine than was obtained from their diet;[9] human studies suggest that a person's diet may be equally or even more important than biosynthesis alone.

Let's now focus our attention on the biochemistry and endogenous synthesis of L-carnitine to get the full picture.

BIOSYNTHESIS OF L-CARNITINE

The chemical structure of L-carnitine is diagramed in Figure 2. The structural formula is called 3-hydroxy-4-N-trimethyl amino butyric acid. Remember, L-carnitine is produced in the kidneys and liver, and the body needs six essential elements for its synthesis: two amino acids (L-lysine and L-methionine) as well as vitamin C, B_6, niacin, and the mineral iron. L-carnitine synthesis begins with the methylation of the amino acid L-lysine by S-adenosyl-L-methionine (SAM).

Figure 2 Chemical Structure of Carnitine

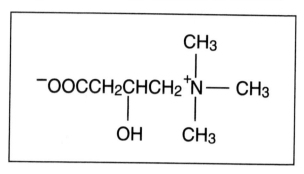

$$^{-}OOCCH_2CHCH_2\overset{+}{N}-CH_3$$

with CH_3 groups and OH as shown

After several more complex steps requiring consecutive methylations and the interaction of several enzymes—and the vitamins and minerals I discussed—carnitine is made in the body. However, it is important to note that dietary deficiencies in L-lysine or in any of the vitamins and minerals mentioned will result in inadequate synthesis of L-carnitine. This is why dietary deficiencies not only of L-carnitine but also the cofactors for biosynthesis are extremely important. These cofactors must be obtained from the diet. It's also important to keep in mind that the higher the dietary intake of carnitine, the greater the increase in the tissue.[10] Like coenzyme Q10, dietary supplementation of L-carnitine increases its levels in the blood and tissues. Now that we've discussed the dietary intake and biosynthesis of L-carnitine, what are its biological functions?

BIOLOGICAL EFFECTS OF L-CARNITINE

The principal function of carnitine is to facilitate the transport of long-chain fatty acids across the inner mitochondrial membrane to begin the process called beta-oxidation (see Figure 1). In fact, L-carnitine is the only carrier that can do this.[11,12] The inner mitochondrial membrane is normally impermeable to activated *coenzyme A (CoA) esters*. Coenzyme A is a very important molecule that binds to many other molecules to make them more reactive and to help transport them across lipid membranes. For example, CoA binds to fatty acids so that beta-oxidation can begin inside the mitochondria. Coenzyme

A esters refer to the molecule that has coenzyme A bound to the fatty acid. These are called *acyl-CoAs.*

In order to enter the inner mitochondrial membrane and then go into the mitochondrial matrix, acyl-CoAs (fats + CoA) require another molecule, L-carnitine. L-carnitine picks up the fatty acid from the acyl-CoA. The acyl-CoA hands off the fat (acyl part) to the carnitine molecule, creating an *acyl-carnitine* molecule, like in a relay race, where the baton is passed from one runner to another. The baton in this case is the fatty acid (acyl). The acyl-carnitine derivative then gets transported, with the help of enzymes called *carnitine acyl transferases,* into the mitochondrial matrix to begin beta-oxidation.

The product of beta-oxidation, *acetyl-CoA,* enters the energy pathway called the *Krebs cycle.* This cycle removes electrons from fatty acids; the electrons then travel through the electron transport chain, with the help of coenzyme Q10, and ultimately make ATP in a process called *oxidative phosphorylation.* Remember, coenzyme Q10 is crucial to generate ATP, and L-carnitine acts like a freight train, bringing the fatty acids into the mitochondria where they are burned in the process called beta-oxidation.

You see, without L-carnitine, fatty acids cannot penetrate through the inner mitochondrial membrane. The rate of beta-oxidation also is determined by how much carnitine is available. Thus, increased levels of carnitine enhance the oxidation effect, while low levels impair it. Because L-carnitine is essential to metabolize most fats, some researchers believe that it may be used as a weight loss aid, particularly when combined with coenzyme Q10 and *chromium,* which helps break down sugars and triglycerides. Another important function of the carnitine shuttle is removal of acetyl units from inside the mitochondria.[13]

This carnitine property also is important because when too many acetyl units accumulate inside the mitochondria, they can disturb the metabolic burning of fats. Other crucial functions of carnitine include the metabolism of branched-chain amino acids, ammonia detoxification, and lactate clearance. Lactate clearance is especially important because high levels of lactic acid (its breakdown product) have been shown to be deleterious to vital tissues such as the heart and the brain. Strenuous exercise can result in high levels of lactic acid, which makes the blood and tissues too acidic. I can remember as a college wrestler the exhaustion I experienced after wrestling nine-minute matches. Sometimes, I was extremely weak, exhausted, and even disoriented following matches that went into overtime. Once I even walked over to the other team's bench and sat down!

I didn't know it back then, but L-carnitine would have been a vital nutrient to take to help clear lactic acid from my blood and tissues.

In one study, for example, a rise in blood lactic acid after exercise was significantly reduced in a carnitine-treated group.[14] Carnitine's ability to remove lactic acid from the blood and tissues helps promote ATP production, and helps avoid the exhaustion that comes from strenuous physical and athletic activity. If I were coaching a wrestling team, I would have every athlete take carnitine, especially since it has been shown to enhance performance.

Ammonia is another toxic by-product of protein metabolism that frequently is a factor in exercise-induced fatigue. Carnitine helps to combat ammonia poisoning by converting ammonia to urea, which is excreted in the urine. In one animal study, for example, toxic doses of ammonia were administered to one group of mice that was pretreated with carnitine and one group that was not. All the mice pretreated with carnitine survived; none of the control animals not treated with carnitine survived.[15]

Lastly, carnitine is considered an antioxidant and free radical scavenger, and has the ability to chelate iron.[16] So, the physiological roles of L-carnitine are quite diverse, offering many ways to enhance many of the metabolic functions of the body. A summary of these attributes is listed in Table 2.

Table 2   The Physiological Benefits of L-Carnitine

Mitochondrial oxidation of long-chain fatty acids	Because the inner mitochondrial membrane is impermeable to the acyl-CoA, L-carnitine is essential for the transfer of long-chain fatty acids from the cytoplasm to the mitochondria, where they undergo beta-oxidation and consequent energy production.

Scavenger system for acyl groups	L-carnitine shuttles fats into the mitochondria, passes them to CoA, and then carries the final products of beta-oxidation out of the matrix, thus increasing cell energy reserves and preventing the accumulation of acetyl groups.
Lactate clearance	L-carnitine plays a role in the removal of lactic acid from blood and tissues and induces a more rapid recovery to the resting value of lactate to pyruvate ratio, which is a measure of aerobic recovery.
Metabolism of branched-chain amino acids	L-carnitine is involved in the formation and utilization of ketone bodies, contributes to the activation of pyruvate-dehydrogenase, and is involved in the metabolism of branched-chain amino acids.
Ammonia detoxification	L-carnitine has a marked protective effect against ammonia poisoning by increasing its conversion into urea, which is subsequently excreted in the urine.
Antioxidant	L-carnitine, and its acyl esters, acetyl-L-carnitine and propionyl-L-carnitine, are free radical scavengers and iron chelators, and may function as antioxidants.

Source: With permission from BIOSINT USA, Inc.

PHARMACOKINETICS AND BIOAVAILABILITY

Since carnitine is made in the human body, there are very few studies that can document how the supplemental use of carnitine is delivered to the tissues. However, after intravenous administration, research data show that carnitine rapidly rises in the blood serum. In one study of healthy volunteers, an intravenous dose of 40 mg/kg demonstrated a peak serum value thirty-six times higher than the baseline concentrations.[17] After oral administration, the peak concentrations were much lower.

Research suggests no significant advantage in supplementing an oral dose of L-carnitine in amounts that exceed 2 grams at any one time because saturation of intestinal mucosa occurs at these higher doses.[18] Maximal blood concentrations are reached in approximately three-and-a-half hours following an oral dose with a half-life of approximately fifteen hours. Because carnitine does not get fully absorbed when taken orally, ingesting it three times a day is the preferred method. Carnitine is eliminated primarily through the kidneys.[19] Like coenzyme Q10, the oral bioavailability of carnitine leaves much to be desired.

Bioavailability refers to the amount of a nutrient that actually gets delivered to the tissues. For example, the dissolution and bioavailability of CoQ10 are poor because it is insoluble in water and poorly soluble in fat. Absorption is difficult unless CoQ10 is accompanied by an excellent delivery system. Research suggests that CoQ10 in a gel results in the best absorption and leads to superior assimilation of the nutrient in the blood.[20] The bioavailability of L-carnitine also is poor. For example, the bioavailability of a 2 gram dose of L-carnitine ranges from 9 percent to 25 percent whereas the bioavailability of a large, 4 to 6 gram dose was only 4 percent to 10 percent, which reflects lower absorption after higher doses. In one clinical study, the estimated bioavailability was approximately 16 percent following a 2 gram dose of L-carnitine.[18]

However, L-Carnitine Fumarate (Sigma-tau, S.p.A., U.S. patent #4,602,039), one of the carnitine salts manufactured by BIO-SINT S.p.A., appears to be absorbed slightly better than L-Carnitine Tartrate. L-Carnitine Fumarate has an available L-carnitine content of 60 percent and a fumaric acid content of 40 percent. Both these substances are natural, are normally present in living organisms, and are metabolized by the human body. In one rodent study, L-Carnitine Fumarate (Sigma-tau) proved to be more bioavailable and also preserved important high-energy phosphate levels during insufficient blood flow to the animals' hearts. L-Carnitine Fumarate (Sigma-tau) also blocked the production of harmful lactate (toxic fatty acids).[21] Thus, it appears that L-Carnitine Fumarate may be one of the best available carnitines for the cardiac patient.

WHY CARNITINE DEFICIENCY?

Although L-carnitine is found throughout the diet and also can be synthesized by your body, research indicates that both primary and secondary deficiencies do occur. It was in 1973 that carnitine deficiencies were first noted in humans; following that discovery extensive case studies in the literature have documented both genetic defects and inborn errors in carnitine metabolism. Now we know that carnitine deficiencies can result from many causes: genetic defects; aging; carnitine-deficient diets (such as seen in pure vegetarians); cofactor deficiencies of vitamin B_6, folic acid, iron, niacin, and especially vitamin C; liver or kidney disease; and the use of certain drugs, particularly anticonvulsant drugs. These deficiencies also can be classified as *myopathic* or *systemic*.

In the myopathic form, the body has normal serum levels of carnitine but reduced skeletal muscle concentrations. People with myopathic carnitine deficiencies usually have symptoms such as muscle fatigue, muscle cramps, and muscle pain following exercise. With systemic carnitine deficiency, both serum and tissue levels of carnitine are abnormally low, and multisystem disturbances are common.[22]

Heart muscle disease, or *cardiomyopathy*, is a common feature in a systemic syndrome. If the heart tissue is examined under a microscope, increased fat deposition and abnormal mitochondria will be seen in the cells. This is where supplemental carnitine has its greatest efficacy.

An example is one young boy with systemic carnitine deficiency. After only one month of approximately 3 grams of carnitine per day, his left ventricular function increased dramatically.[23] (There are also other anecdotal case reports on record.) Secondary carnitine deficiencies are most often associated with renal failure, dialysis, severe malnutrition, and liver cirrhosis. Recently, the AIDS population has shown significantly reduced levels of carnitine. Some of the end-stage symptoms of AIDS—exhaustion, cachexia, and muscle weakness—may respond to carnitine supplementation, offering patients potential therapeutic benefit. Although carnitine deficiencies may occur at very different levels, the more common subtle deficiencies occur in those with cardiovascular disease. So let's discuss what I believe is one organ for which carnitine has the greatest utility: the heart.

L-CARNITINE AND THE HEART

Now that you know about the biochemistry of L-carnitine, you can see why it's so crucial for the cardiac patient. Remember, the primary function of L-carnitine is the transport of fatty acids to the inner mitochondrial membrane where they're burned as fuel. Since the normal heart gets at least 60 percent of its fuel from fat sources,[24] maximizing the oxidation of these fats is especially crucial for anyone with a form of heart disease, particularly people with moderate to severe heart disease.

Those who have moderate to severe atherosclerosis with varying degrees of congestive heart failure (see Table 3) usually are the most physically compromised by their symptoms. The American Heart Association (AHA) identifies these individuals as AHA Class III or AHA Class IV patients (depending upon the severity of their symptoms). Class III and IV patients experience symptoms of moderate to extreme fatigue; shortness of breath on minimal activity or even when lying down (flat); chest discomfort; and swelling of the ankles. All these symptoms are related to the oxygen-starved heart struggling to pump hard enough to keep the blood moving forward. The more extensive the heart disease, the less oxygen is available for work. The weaker the heart becomes, the more we see these problems of blood congestion backing up into the lungs and into the tissues.

I've been delighted to discover that the addition of L-carnitine has had a very positive—and measurable—impact on many of my patients with heart disease. Over the years I have had great results using coenzyme Q10. There were some patients who did not respond, however. Although coenzyme Q10 alone has been effective in approximately 85 percent of my patients, I still was concerned about the other 15 percent whose lives were severely limited by their symptoms.

Table 3   New York Heart Association (NYHA) Classification of Patients with Heart Failure

Class I:	*No limitations:* Ordinary physical activity does not cause undue fatigue, dyspnea (difficult or labored breathing), or palpitations.
Class II:	*Slight limitation of physical activity:* Such patients are comfortable at rest. Ordinary physical activity results in fatigue, palpitations, dyspnea, or angina.
Class III:	*Marked limitation of physical activity:* Although patients are comfortable at rest, less-than-ordinary amounts of activity will lead to symptoms.
Class IV:	*Inability to carry on any physical activity without discomfort:* Symptoms of congestive heart failure are present even at rest. With any physical activity, increased discomfort is experienced.

So I searched the medical literature and found there, too, reports that approximately 12 percent to 15 percent of patients failed to respond to CoQ10 alone, even though they had excellent blood levels of 3.5 ug/ml or higher. How was it, I asked myself, that they seemed unable to take advantage of the CoQ10 in their own bodies?

I was excited to learn that, for many of these refractory patients, the addition of L-carnitine to their nutritional and medical programs seemed to provide an additional boost in energy. It was this challenging patient population that demonstrated to me the efficacy of coenzyme Q10 and L-carnitine in combination.

They say a picture is worth a thousand words—and I agree! When these treatment-resitant folks came in with better color, breathing easier, and walking around the office with minimal difficulty, I was nothing short of amazed! It was as if the L-carnitine provided the powerpack to work in synergism with the CoQ10. That's why I now refer to these two nutrients as the "twin pillars of healing" for the heart. They have changed the way I treat congestive heart failure and ischemic heart disease. Let me explain some of the physiology and the research findings so you can better understand how things work.

The heart is so metabolically active that it requires a constant supply of ATP, the body's main energy source. Cardiac muscle cells burn fats for fuel. But the heart demands such a constant and high level of energy resources to pump—60 to 100 times a minute, twenty-four hours a day for years and years—that it's especially vulnerable to even subtle deficiencies in the factors contributing to ATP production: coenzyme Q10 and L-carnitine.

In fact, tissue deficiencies of both coenzyme Q10 and L-carnitine have been noted in people with heart disease.[25] One research group studied eleven patients with chronic rheumatic heart disease (RHD) who had valve and muscle damage that required valve replacement.[26] Their average myocardial free-carnitine levels were found to be 0.72 +/-0.37 mu mol per gram (dry weight), compared to ten "relatively healthy" matched control patients who were undergoing coronary artery bypass surgery; their mean levels were 1.44 plus or minus 1.03 mu mol per gram (dry weight). As you can see, the long-standing chronic demand in the RHD group had stripped their nutrient levels down to only one-half.

Luckily for us, our heart muscle is one of the most responsive organs in the body for targeted nutritional supplementation. This fact makes practicing "nutritional cardiology" a must for me! In addition to vitamin E, and the plethora of nutrients that can benefit the heart, I feel it's important to focus on the "twin pillar" cardioprotective nutrients, because they've been so helpful across such a wide spectrum of cardiac conditions. My personal experience as well as the scientific literature support L-carnitine and coenzyme Q10 as being effective in a wide variety of cardiovascular situations. Examples include:

1. Angina pectoris
2. Unstable angina
3. Congestive heart failure
4. Toxin-induced cardiotoxicity (a common side-effect of Adriamycin®)
5. Renal insufficiency, especially on those having dialysis
6. Ventricular arrhythmia
7. High cholesterol and lipid disorders
8. Peripheral claudication (leg cramps)

As you can see from this long list, L-carnitine is a heart-specific supplement you can't afford *not* to consider if you have any of these cardiac conditions. Together with its derivative, *propionyl-L-carnitine*, L-carnitine is a key nutrient for cardiac tissue. These cofactors not only enhance free fatty acid metabolism but also pack an extra punch to reduce the intracellular buildup of toxic metabolites—particularly in situations where the heart muscle is not getting enough oxygen. I couldn't practice cardiology without them!

I am so used to dealing with the side effects of cardiac drugs that I can't tell you how much better I sleep at night prescribing nutrients like the carnitines, which are virtually devoid of any significant side effect. Since the majority of cardiac patients are recovering from a heart attack or struggling with angina, I'd like you to understand these two cardiovascular diseases in more detail.

ANGINA AND HEART ATTACK

UNDERSTANDING ANGINA

Simply stated, *angina* is a "heart cramp." Anginal symptoms are caused by an insufficient supply of oxygen to the heart tissues, usually resulting from blockages and/or spasms of the coronary arteries. Typically, patients understand the term *angina* to describe squeezing, pressure, or even burning discomfort in the chest, or pain that may travel from shoulder to shoulder or up into the neck, occasionally radiating into the back and left arm.

But it's important to know that many people experience their angina as shortness of breath, as the body attempts to pull in more oxygen to compensate for the shortage. This symptom may be the only warning for someone with diabetes, because their nerve endings may be less sensitive to other signs. Some of the symptoms of angina can be less typical, such as soreness or pain in the jaw, a tooth, the back, or the forearms.

Whatever the symptoms of angina in any particular case,

the cause is oxygen deprivation in the heart muscle. This is usually the result of coronary arteries that have become blocked over time from a buildup of cholesterol-laden plaque. Most of you are familiar with this process, thanks to the public awareness of our number-one killer. You also may know that this condition usually progresses with age.

As these blockages increase in size, they crowd the artery opening, or *lumen,* and limit the flow of oxygen to the heart muscle. Remember, it's the lack of oxygen to the cardiac tissue that causes the symptoms. It's like applying a tourniquet around your thigh. If it's not eventually released, numbness, pain, and discoloration will occur. The same thing happens in your heart. You can't see it, but the symptoms will let you know that something is going wrong. That's good, because otherwise you might push your heart too far.

What can trigger episodes of angina? Common culprits are intense cold, physical exertion, emotional stress, excessive heat, or an over-reactive thyroid. Occasionally coronary artery spasm occurs; this, too, squeezes the lumen shut and contributes to a reduction in oxygen delivery. For some people, angina is the result of a combination of coronary artery spasm and underlying plaque. These are the most irritable areas of your arteries because the inner walls, or *intima,* can become seriously inflamed from atherosclerosis.

Physicians use the term *stable angina* to describe a fixed relationship between oxygen supply and demand. Stable angina generally is easier to treat. In fact, stable angina is commonly reproducible using treadmill stress testing. Symptoms occur with exertion, usually from a particular workload. But the hormones released with emotional stress—like adrenalin and cortisol—also can push up heart rate and blood pressure and trigger artery spasm. Emotional stress is harder to quantify and regulate, however.

We use the term *unstable angina* when episodes aren't predictable. *Unstable angina* is provoked more frequently, lasts longer, and even can occur during rest or sleep, when there is no extra oxygen demand on the heart. Basically angina, whether unstable or stable, is related to cardiac economics: Whatever the cause, the heart's demand for oxygen has outstripped its supply.

When treating someone with angina, the physician's goal is to raise what we call the *anginal threshold,* the point at which the symptom cuts in like an unwanted dance partner, limiting the amount of activity one can perform. The last time I checked, no one was raising their hand for more limitations on their lifestyle—we want to be able to do *more!*

TRADITIONAL TREATMENT FOR ANGINA

Cardiologists frequently use medications to protect the heart muscle from high oxygen demand. Some drugs work to reduce the heart's workload and oxygen demand by lowering blood pressure or heart rate. Medications such as nitroglycerin, and other nitrates, work directly on the arterial walls, causing them to widen or dilate. This, in turn, increases the supply of oxygen to the heart muscle. These agents usually allow anginal patients to increase their activity level without provoking symptoms.

The major classes of drugs used to reduce symptoms of coronary artery disease are *nitrates, beta blockers, calcium channel blockers, ACE inhibitors,* and *blood thinners,* such as aspirin. Drug therapy certainly has a definitive place in the treatment of coronary artery disease by offering improved quality of life for many people with heart blockages who don't really need coronary artery bypass surgery. These medications also offer symptom relief to patients as they tackle risk factors in order to slow down the progression of the disease.

But frequently these drugs can't improve the oxygen demand/supply ratio. In such cases, blood flow needs to be increased more directly, by an invasive procedure. It is at this point that the cardiologist may recommend *percutaneous transluminal coronary angioplasty (PTCA)* or may ask a surgeon to evaluate the patient for *coronary artery bypass surgery (CABS)* to reroute blood flow to the heart. As a cardiologist, I believe in the appropriateness of all these interventions; drug and surgical therapies have potential benefits and do improve the quality of life for many people.

These treatment options can have unpleasant side effects, however. That's why L-carnitine is so important to me and the way I practice medicine. Cardioprotective supplements offer a more conservative, additional therapy option to my patients, especially those struggling with therapeutic side effects or making a decision about PTCA or CABS procedures. And they may be just what's needed to get anginal symptoms under control or to give extra protection if an invasive intervention is scheduled. Like coenzyme Q10, L-carnitine is another gift to the cardiology patient. Now let me explain how L-carnitine can help alleviate the symptoms of angina.

L-CARNITINE AND ANGINA

There are plenty of double-blind, placebo-controlled research studies in the cardiovascular literature that show the efficacy of L-carnitine—and its cousin, *propionyl-L-carnitine*—in treating angina, as well as in treating other cardiovascular disorders. (Be aware that you will find several carnitines under scrutiny if you check the literature.) The results are convincing. Because propionyl-L-carnitine is taken up by myocardial cells more readily than other forms of carnitine, several studies evaluated this carnitine and its effect on the heart. *Acetyl-L-carnitine,* which is taken up more widely by the brain, is the best studied form of all the carnitines for brain health and fitness.

But for our discussion, I want to focus on L-carnitine. It's the most widely available and least expensive of all forms of carnitines, so it's probably the one you'll be thinking of taking. What is it about carnitine that makes it a critical adjunct to the proper functioning of the human heart, especially in the clinical setting of angina?

Carnitine enhances fatty acid metabolism and prevents the accumulation of toxic fatty acid metabolites inside cardiac tissue. It is beneficial in angina because it improves overall oxygen utilization by the heart cells.[27] Starved heart muscle cells need to utilize the limited oxygen supply more effectively; carnitine helps reduce that demand by burning other fuel sources, such as fats. All forms of commercial carnitine have been demonstrated to be useful in treating angina.[28,29] Investigating the relationship of angina and carnitine has been done in several experimental models, including exercise studies and stress studies done using human hearts with pacemakers.

Leading the clinical research on carnitine in angina were

investigations in the experimental animal model. These data suggested that L-carnitine was beneficial in limiting angina, or *myocardial ischemia*, due to its metabolic effect. *Ischemia* is defined as lack of oxygenated blood flow to a tissue. There's a vicious cycle that takes place during ischemic episodes, which actually makes things worse. Even before the person may be aware of an anginal symptom, several metabolic abnormalities occur almost instantaneously: beta-oxidation is curtailed, and toxic high levels of free fatty acids start accumulating. There's an intracellular accumulation of the fatty acid metabolite, acetyl-CoA, which further impairs myocardial function. All these nasty by-products paralyze the mitochondria, which become dysfunctional. Then, ATP levels crash. What a mess! It's like fanning a fire with a gasoline-soaked towel!

Early research suggested that carnitine provided protection against the medical consequences of ischemia. Investigators have confirmed this finding and have expanded the work to validate its positive effect on other cardiovascular disorders.[30] Usually, anginal symptoms are triggered by an increase in physical workload. So, a great way to study the impact of carnitine in individuals with angina is to use exercise studies.

In a study by Kamikawa and colleagues,[31] a low dose of 900 mg daily of L-carnitine was associated with an improvement in exercise tolerance in patients with "effort angina." The test results also showed a longer exercise time during the period of carnitine therapy. The average time required for 1 mm of *ST segment depression* (EKG evidence for ischemia) was 6.4 minutes during the placebo period. This was extended to a mean of 8.8 minutes after twelve weeks of carnitine treatment. It's interesting to note that, of the twelve patients who experienced angina during the placebo period, two of them were angina free after three months of treatment with carnitine. I've found myself speculating that if the researchers had used higher doses of carnitine—perhaps closer to the 2 and 3 gram daily doses given today—an even greater difference in exercise time/symptom relief might have been realized.

In a more recent controlled study, the therapeutic effect of L-carnitine was evaluated at three different centers in 200 patients, forty to sixty-five years of age, with documented exercise-induced angina.[32] After patients received their usual drug regimen and daily doses of 2 grams of L-carnitine, they were compared with controls over a six-month period. The experimental group not only showed a significant reduction in *ventricular ectopic contractions* (cardiac skipped beats) but also exhibited an increased tolerance on cycle exercise, an increased double cardiac product (heart rate × blood pressure) and a reduced ST segment response on EKG (less ischemia).

These parameters demonstrate improved cardiac performance for those receiving the L-carnitine. Researchers also documented participants' reports that their quality of life improved. Amazingly, this improvement was observed in patients who were the lowest on the New York Heart Association functional charts. It may be that those whose bodies are most depleted in these nutrients have the most to gain from supplementation. Many researchers are asking themselves, "What is it about L-carnitine? Why do patients show an improvement in their anginal symptoms with the addition of L-carnitine? Is there more to understand?"

Thomsen and colleagues[33] reported in *The American Journal of Cardiology* that the intravenous administration of L-carnitine improved the cardiac-pacing tolerance in ischemic human hearts. In other words, when pacing wires were positioned in the heart and the heart rate was increased by electrical stimulation, patients could tolerate higher heart rate ranges without angina if they had been pretreated with intravenous carnitine. These researchers also measured *myocardial lactate metabolism* and found that the condition improved in the presence of carnitine. Remember, increased lactate can be toxic to the normal functioning of the heart. These results, too, suggest that carnitine is doing something to improve the metabolism in the ischemic zones of the myocardium.

Next, we'll be looking at other chronic and acute ischemic heart conditions where carnitine levels also may be depleted: heart attack and heart failure.[34,35] Later, I'll discuss other cardioprotective effects that occur when carnitine is supplemented, such as a reduction in total cholesterol and triglyceride levels. It's these combinations of heart health effects that suggest L-carnitine is a "home run player" in the management of cardiac risk, angina, and ischemic heart disease.

I just want to emphasize that carnitine's mode of action differs from that of other antianginal agents which cardiologists use. Like coenzyme Q10, L-carnitine can safely and effectively be taken in combination with beta blockers, calcium blockers, nitrates, and ACE inhibitors, for a more full-spectrum approach to symptom relief.

So, for anyone with angina, it's possible to theorize that myocardial stores of carnitine may be diminished due to chronic, episodic bouts of ischemia. The supplemental use of L-carnitine by the angina patient also may delay the shift from *aerobic* to *anaerobic* metabolism. Less anaerobic metabolism translates into a reduction in its metabolite, lactate, a culprit agent in the vicious angina syndrome. So let's move on, because, for those with suspected heart attack, L-carnitine's protective qualities are worth knowing about!

CARNITINE AND ACUTE MYOCARDIAL INFARCTION

When a blood clot forms and gets stuck in a coronary artery, it's a disaster! These clots probably originate at a plaque site where platelets stick and attach themselves. This is often the start of an *acute coronary* or a *heart attack*—what we used to call a *coronary thrombosis*. Now we use the term *myocardial infarction* (myo = muscle, cardio = heart, infarction = tissue death), or *MI*, to denote a heart attack.

Sometimes the clot forms somewhere else, becomes stuck at a place it can't get through, and that's your blocked coronary artery. Or maybe an episode of spasm lasts so long that the blood congeals in a relatively open area of the arterial circulation (a rare occurrence). Wherever the clot came from, once it jams itself in a coronary artery, it's an emergency! Only a little blood, or no blood at all, is able to trickle through to the desperate tissue downstream. Without blood and the life-saving oxygen it carries, heart muscle will die, and maybe the patient will, too. One-half of all heart attack victims won't make it. That's a tough statistic we battle every day.

One group of researchers decided to see what help carnitine could provide in this acute situation. If it worked in angina, maybe there was a role for carnitine in emergency cardiology. In another randomized double-blind, placebo-controlled trial, the effects of 2 grams of L-carnitine were compared to placebo in 101 patients with suspected heart attack. The treatment period lasted four weeks. At the end of the twenty-eight-day protocol, the area of tissue damage was assessed. Infarct size was found to be significantly reduced in the carnitine group compared to its matched controls.[36]

In addition to limiting tissue damage, there was also a reduction in *ischemic arrhythmias* and in heart enlargement. Unfortunately, there was also a difference in mortality: more deaths noted in the placebo group. The researchers concluded that L-carnitine may protect cardiac tissue as well as prevent cardiac complications of heart attack, including fatality.

In a recent placebo-controlled study reported in the *Journal of the American College of Cardiology*,[37] researchers confirmed that giving carnitine after an acute heart attack had a beneficial effect on the preservation of the left ventricle (LV), where most heart damage occurs, by preventing an increase in heart size. This has enormous treatment implications because, during the first year after a heart attack, an increase in LV size is an ominously powerful predictor of future adverse cardiac events.

Looking at the total picture, we can see that L-carnitine supplementation has enormous potential to protect heart attack survivors. Although the latter trial included 472 patients with their first heart attack—a good-size cohort from which to draw conclusions—a larger, double-blind trial should be considered in the future, using mortality as a specific clinical end point. However, based on the results of these two recent studies, L-carnitine, like coenzyme Q10, should be considered by every reputable cardiologist who wishes to improve his patients' quality of life and survival rate.

Speaking of survival, perhaps the most outstanding aspect of the use of L-carnitine supplementation in cardiovascular conditions has been its ability to assist coenzyme Q10 in reducing the mortality from end-stage congestive heart failure. We shall discuss this impressive data in the next section.

CONGESTIVE HEART FAILURE

One of the major advances in cardiovascular disease over the last two decades has been the reduction in coronary heart attack, probably as a result of tremendous risk factor modification. But during the same twenty-year period, deaths from heart failure have more than doubled. To look into this problem, 159 of the nation's leading cardiologists met regularly during the past one-and-a-half years. They found that most heart failure patients are routinely treated with two drugs: *digitalis* (Lanoxin®, digoxin) to help slow the heart so it can fill and empty better and increase the strength of its contractions; and a *diuretic* (Lasix®, Bumex®, Aldactone®) to help the body rid itself of excess salt and water.

Patients and doctors alike have applauded these drugs because they offer immediate relief of symptoms like shortness of breath, swollen ankles, and even chest pressure and discomfort. The problem is that, while many people do feel better on this regimen, the underlying heart problem rarely is improved, and frequently progresses. Today cardiologists may recommend other drugs such as an ACE inhibitor and beta blockers. These agents help reduce some of the stress on the heart, allowing it to pump more effectively by relaxing arteries and lowering blood pressure. However, although these drugs may improve symptoms, they really don't get to the "heart of the matter," either. It's like giving aspirin for a headache: The pain is gone, but do we know *why* you had the headache? And, can we prevent another one?

We have to keep in mind that, in congestive heart failure, there are insufficient myocardial contractive forces to make the heart an effective pump. And since pumping is number one on the heart's agenda, inadequate pulsatile forces mean the heart is not strong enough to pump the blood around the body. That's why people become congested, why their ankles swell and their lungs fill up with fluid.

Congestive heart failure literally is an energy-starved heart. So one way to attack this problem is to give nutritional supports that can supply the heart with the additional energy it needs to strengthen cardiac contractions. This is where the "twin pillars of healing" come into play. Both L-carnitine and coenzyme Q10 support the bioenergetic processes of the heart: They enhance ATP production and promote more efficient metabolism in the mitochondria.

Each myocardial cell can have 5,000 mitochondria supporting energy reserves. By improving mitochondrial function with L-carnitine and coenzyme Q10, the energy-starved heart becomes a more effective pump, offering you a better quality of life and enhancing your survival.

One of the major problems that cardiologists face in treating *congestive heart failure (CHF)* is fighting the high mortality rate. Patients with CHF may have had multiple heart attacks, resulting in so much scar tissue that the amount of healthy, functioning muscle is limited. Others may have *cardiomyopathy,* a condition in which the heart muscle has become dilated, stretched out, and enlarged, often as the result of long-standing high blood pressure. Other cases of CHF may result from valvular problems, viruses that have attacked the heart muscle, or generalized atherosclerosis. And all too often, CHF and cardiomyopathy are *idiopathic,* meaning we really don't know for sure what caused them. (We'll talk more about that in the next section.)

Because the root causes can be so varied, or so vague, cardiologists not only should use conventional drugs for treating their patients, they also should consider adding powerful nutritional supports from resources like L-carnitine, coenzyme Q10, and magnesium. They then will be treating symptoms as well as directing nutrition to the cellular level where it can make a real difference in the underlying pathology. I have found that the simple addition of these three nutrients has impacted my patients' quality of life most positively and has helped them live longer with their condition. Let's review some of the clinical research on CHF and L-carnitine.

In a controlled study of 160 patients hospitalized for heart attack, eighty patients received 4 grams of L-carnitine daily for twelve months. The other eighty received placebo, and both groups continued their conventional pharmacological treatments. All subjects noticed improvements in arterial blood pressure, cholesterol levels, rhythm disorders, and signs and symptoms of congestive heart failure. But the most significant finding was the tremendous reduction in mortality for the carnitine-supplemented subjects: 1.2 percent compared to 12.5 percent for the controls![38]

More recently, Singh and colleagues performed a double-blind, placebo-controlled trial on 100 patients with suspected myocardial infarction.[39] Experimental subjects received 2 grams of L-carnitine a day for twenty-eight days. Supplemented participants showed an improvement in arrhythmia, angina, heart failure, and mean infarct size, as well as a reduction in total cardiac events, including cardiac deaths. There was a significant reduction in cardiac death and non-fatal infarction in the carnitine group: 15.6 percent as compared to 26 percent in the placebo group. Although a larger study may be useful in the future to confirm this research, the fact remains that the addition of L-carnitine improved several end points, including subsequent cardiac events, without any toxic effects.

In the European study of 472 patients published in the *Journal of the American College of Cardiology*, intravenous carnitine at a dose of 9 grams daily for five days was followed by 6 grams orally for the next twelve months.[40] These investigators again validated previous studies, demonstrating an improvement in ejection fraction (EF) and a reduction in left ventricular size in carnitine-treated patients. (*Ejection fraction* is the proportion of blood that's pumped out of the heart on each heartbeat. Most of the time, the heart is able to pump out 55 to 75 percent of the incoming blood, and the rest just sloshes back. In CHF, the EF is often reduced, sometimes as low as 10 to 15 percent in severe cases.)

Although the European study was not designed to demonstrate differences in clinical end points, the combined incidence of CHF death after discharge was 6 percent in the L-carnitine treatment group versus 9.6 percent in placebo group, a reduction of more than 30 percent.

In a small Japanese study of nine patients with congestive heart failure, five patients (55 percent) moved to a lower NYHA class, and the overall condition was improved in six patients (66 percent), after treatment with a daily dose of only 900 mg of L-carnitine.[41] Although these patients had improved symptoms, there was no significant improvement on echocardiographic parameters. This is a finding I frequently face when I employ coenzyme Q10, L-carnitine, or the two in combination. Frequently patients do report a marked improvement in their physical symptoms: less shortness of breath, less fatigue, less ankle swelling, more energy, better sleep, and increased appetite. It's confusing that there's no "hard evidence" of improved cardiodynamics using echocardiographic evaluation; for example, there may not appear to be any increase in ejection fraction, although one would expect it.

We must keep in mind that both L-carnitine and CoQ10 promote energy to *cardiac myocytes* (muscle cells). It's important to note that this action is physiological and is not similar to the pharmacological actions of drugs that affect heart rate and contractility of the heart. So why do patients with heart failure improve on L-carnitine?

Since endocardial biopsies taken from patients with chronic heart failure have shown a decrease in ATP concentration and impairment of myocardial contraction, it's now believed that serious defects in the metabolism of heart cells is present in chronic CHF.[42] Since there's a loss of free carnitine and an increase in long-chained acyl carnitine in the heart cells of weakened hearts, L-carnitine supplementation may improve mitochondrial dynamics and in turn improve myocardial oxygen uptake and use.

This is why it's crucial for cardiologists treating heart failure to think in terms of *energy expenditure* and *energy economics*. Efforts must be directed toward more targeted treatments—treatments that can get directly into the cell, not just work to reduce "pre-load" and "after-load," the opposing forces that work against and strain the heart muscle. We have drugs to target the external forces that weaken the heart, but nutritional supplementation with the "twin pillars" offers a solution that assists the energy-starved mitochondria. Only by allowing them to live up to their nickname, the "powerhouses of the cell," can we target our treatment to the cells in need. By supporting energy expenditure and boosting oxygen utilization, physicians can offer CHF patients a solution that gets to the core of the problem. They not only may feel better, they may live longer, too. That's what I call a "total attack" on the problem!

PERIPHERAL VASCULAR DISEASE, ARRHYTHMIA, LIPID DISORDERS, AND ADRIAMYCIN TOXICITY

PERIPHERAL VASCULAR DISEASE

Many of my patients with heart disease also have more generalized circulation problems. A condition called *intermittent claudication* mimics angina, but the pain occurs in the calf muscle instead of the heart. Like angina, the pain of claudication is described as a cramp or tightness. This discomfort and pain can occur with simple, everyday activities, like walking around the house or shopping. For them, daily life is circumscribed by the limitations of their ability to walk. You may know exactly what I mean if you've had a bypass operation on your heart, only to discover that your legs started holding you back once your cardiac limitations were lifted!

The pain you experienced is due to reduced oxygen delivery to your legs, which, in turn, encourages increased production of free radicals. No wonder it hurts! In fact, these two circulatory problems coexist so often that if you (or someone you know) has leg claudication and has not been evaluated for heart disease, a good cardiac checkup is a must. L-carnitine works for claudication symptoms the same way it works for angina. Even though carnitine doesn't have a direct effect on your blood flow (it doesn't widen the artery like nitroglycerin), it can improve cellular energy production if your blood flow is compromised. It even can improve the efficiency of the skeletal muscles in your peripheral tissues, by bolstering them to extract additional oxygen in times of exertional demand. Remember, skeletal muscle, like heart muscle, requires the oxidation of fatty acids as an important energy source.

Just as patients with angina have pain in the heart during activity, patients with *peripheral vascular disease (PVD)* develop skeletal muscle ischemia upon exertion. But what is the biochemical basis for these symptoms?

To begin with, we know that skeletal muscle metabolism may be altered by poor perfusion of blood in the leg. People with PVD develop ischemia in their legs during exercise because of obstructed blood flow in a large artery, like the femoral or popliteal. Symptoms of intermittent claudication are experienced when walking as little as 50 or 100 feet. When there is muscle ischemia or lack of blood flow, there is impaired metabolism; the result is an accumulation of metabolic intermediaries that can worsen the situation.

To test this theory, a study of eleven patients with PVD was performed to demonstrate the relationship between ischemia and the formation of acyl carnitine. The PVD subjects were compared to eleven age-matched controls without PVD. All subjects walked on a treadmill to an end point of either pain or, in the control group, to a maximal workload. Patients with PVD demonstrated an increase in plasma long-chain acyl carnitine at peak exercise, which persisted for four minutes.[43] Their ankle blood pressure also was reduced although they continued to experience pain, which suggests that an increase in the formation of acyl carnitine may reflect changes in metabolic activity, resulting in the symptoms of ischemia.

Researchers hypothesized that the conversion of carnitine to acyl carnitine might serve as a marker of metabolic events that occur in ischemic muscle. So the question is, Could the supplementation of L-carnitine support the vulnerable peripheral muscle during episodes of compromised blood flow? Although only a few studies have been performed in patients with PVD, the data results seen with supplemental carnitine are encouraging.

For example, in one trial with a double-blind cross-over design, twenty patients with PVD were treated with either placebo or 4 grams of L-carnitine for three weeks.[44] In the group receiving carnitine, there was a 75 percent greater walking capacity compared to those receiving placebo. Carnitine also reduced many subjective complaints such as tiredness, numbness, and pain while walking, whereas placebo had only a minimal effect on these subjective symptoms. How does carnitine make such a substantial improvement?

The researchers again speculated that carnitine had a metabolic effect rather than a regional hemodynamic effect (blood pressure or heart rate). Carnitine did inhibit increases in venous lactate concentrations while driving pyruvate oxidation for enhanced energy. In essence, L-carnitine supplementation helps to maximize efficient metabolic activity by mobilizing ATP and promoting better utilization of oxygen. A similar type of reasoning can be applied to arrhythmia, another condition of the heart that has been found to respond to both coenzyme Q10 and L-carnitine.

CARDIAC ARRHYTHMIA

Cardiac palpitations are one of the most common problems that bring patients to a cardiologist's office. Two of the most benign yet frequent types are PVCs and PACs. *Premature ventricular contractions (PVCs)* and *premature atrial contractions (PACs)* represent heartbeats that come early in the cardiac cycle. The individual may experience an early beat, which is followed by a pause that often is described as a *palpitation*. What actually happens is that the premature ectopic beat occurs, and then is followed by a pause that feels like a "skip." In reality, the slight pause is allowing more blood to enter the heart so that the next, normal contraction feels more pronounced. This creates the sensation that the heart is palpitating.

A PVC happens when the ectopic beat originates in the left or right ventricle of the heart. Similarly, a PAC occurs when the "out-of-synch" beat is initiated somewhere in the atria. There are many causes for PACs and PVCs: stimulants like coffee and alcohol; excessive sugars; lack of oxygen; mitral valve prolapse; stress and anxiety; low potassium/low magnesium states; and sometimes medications.

Generally speaking, most cardiologists do not treat infrequent PACs or PVCs with drugs, since most of these rhythm disturbances occur in healthy hearts. However, some patients are quite symptomatic and do require some form of therapy. Fortunately, there are some excellent nutritional supports, which can help prevent palpitations. My typical "cocktail" for suppressing PACs or PVCs includes a combination of coenzyme, L-carnitine, and magnesium. Remember that the accumulation of toxic fatty acid metabolites can cause considerable cardiac compromise. Not only can these by-products weaken the contraction of the heart and make you more vulnerable to irregular heartbeats, these toxic metabolites eventually can also injure cardiac tissue. But by supplementing with L-carnitine, you can put a major dent in these scary processes and help your heart "keep the beat" energetically, as it was meant to. But why are these toxic fatty acid compounds so disturbing to your heartbeat?

Researchers believe that these toxic fatty acid metabolites are so damaging because they disrupt cellular membranes, which in turn interrupt the stable environment for electrical transmission of impulses. It's the changes in these cellular membranes throughout the heart cells that are thought to contribute to impaired contraction of the heart muscle, and thus to an increased vulnerability to irregular heartbeats. Let's look at some of the research in the animal model on L-carnitine and its impact on *ventricular arrhythmia*.

We know from previous research that high concentrations of free fatty acids have been known to trigger arrhythmias, particularly in a setting of ischemic heart disease.[45] Perhaps you've heard the term *café coronary*? This term is used to describe a seemingly calm setting of a high-fat meal, plus a little alcohol and a touch of unresolved stress—a common scenario for a heart attack that takes place during a social dinner. Although there are several simultaneous variables going on in this café drama, I'd like to emphasize the accumulation of toxic free fatty acid intermediates and their direct effect on your myocardial cells.

In one experimental animal study, ischemic hearts demonstrated an excessive surge in free fatty acids after eighty minutes of coronary occlusion, while at the same time levels of free carnitine and ATP were decreased.[46] In the treatment groups, long-chain acyl carnitines and free fatty acid increases were reduced by the addition of L-carnitine. Pretreatment of L-carnitine also reduced more serious arrhythmias in this animal model, leading researchers to suggest that carnitine may be beneficial in arrhythmias, presumably by supporting free fatty acid metabolism.

I have seen impressive results in my own clinical experience with patients responding to L-carnitine, particularly in combination with coenzyme Q10, magnesium, potassium, calcium, and an herb called hawthorn berry. Frequently, with the aid of these synergistic combinations, I also have been able to reduce patients' use of some of the conventional drugs we use to suppress these arrhythmias. In fact, the human research on L-carnitine alone is intriguing.

The antiarrhythmic potential of carnitine has been evaluated in some human clinical studies, as well. In one double-blind study, the effect of carnitine on ventricular arrhythmia was studied in patients with acute heart attack.[47] The fifty-six subjects were randomly assigned to receive infusions of 100 mg/kg of L-carnitine or placebo every twelve hours for a total of thirty-six hours. The study demonstrated that premature ventricular ectopic beats, as well as the number of high-grade ventricular tachycardias (malignant arrhythmias), were significantly lower in the patients treated with L-carnitine than in those receiving placebo. The protective antiarrhythmic effects were accompanied by higher serum levels of free carnitine, confirming absorption and reflecting the impact of supplementation. Similar findings have been seen in other controlled studies.

One European study involved thirty-eight elderly patients with congestive heart failure who were taking traditional medical therapies, including digitalis, diuretics, and antiarrhythmic agents. Twenty-one of them were treated with oral L-carnitine at a dose of 1 gram twice daily for forty-five days.[48] The seventeen controls were placed on placebo. Although both groups demonstrated improvement in NYHA classes, the L-carnitine group experienced a significant reduction in the incidence of cardiac arrhythmias, particularly premature ventricular contractions (PVCs). There also was a decrease in digoxin requirements for the L-carnitine group. This study not only justified the use of L-carnitine in patients with congestive heart failure, but it also justified its use as adjunct therapy in patients with cardiac arrhythmia. Again, the carnitine deficiencies documented in these patients may reflect toxic intermediary metabolites such as acyl carnitine, which are known to enhance the possibility of arrhythmia.

Another special population in which carnitine depletion may occur includes those undergoing renal dialysis. These individuals are also extremely vulnerable to ventricular arrhythmia.

CARNITINE AND KIDNEY DISEASE

The loss of carnitine in the *dialysate* (dialysis solution) may result in carnitine deficiency, setting the stage for the development of cardiac arrhythmias. When patients undergo renal dialysis, the small carnitine molecule is quite readily lost or "washed out" by the dialysate. We have to be mindful that a diseased kidney may not synthesize enough carnitine. The kidney is a *major* site of carnitine biosynthesis, so any diseased kidney is a threat to carnitine production.

Patients with renal failure who are undergoing hemodialysis often experience muscle weakness, high triglyceride levels, congestive heart failure, and cardiac arrhythmias. A carnitine deficiency in these patients is a likely occurrence and should always be suspected when these symptoms occur.

It's well known that many patients on chronic dialysis experience cardiac arrhythmias, usually a short time after beginning the procedure. This often occurs after the patient is given the blood thinner called *heparin*, which often results in a rise in free fatty acid levels. In one study involving a small group of patients, there was significant reduction in the frequency of ventricular arrhythmias in those treated with 2 grams of L-carnitine the day before the start of the dialysis procedure. Carnitine therapy resulted in an increase in plasma carnitine and a corresponding reduction in free fatty acids. Treated subjects also had a lower incidence of severe arrhythmia.[49]

It's clear that patients undergoing hemodialysis are at risk for developing a carnitine deficiency; therefore, dietitians, physicians, and other health-care professionals need to be especially aware of the valuable benefits of L-carnitine supplementation for this vulnerable group.[50] Carnitine deficiency in this population of patients also has implications for treatment of high triglyceride and cholesterol levels.

CARNITINE: TRIGLYCERIDES AND CHOLESTEROL

One of the risk factors for patients undergoing hemodialysis is *hypertriglyceridemia*. Because carnitine deficiencies can result in impaired fatty acid oxidation, hypertriglyceridemia is commonly triggered. The result is that the patient becomes even more vulnerable to developing atherosclerosis. In one study, twenty-nine hemodialysis patients with hypertriglyceridemia were treated with L-carnitine. Twelve patients showed a reduction in triglyceride levels, while seventeen showed no decrease.[51] The patients who responded not only had high levels of triglycerides but low levels of HDL cholesterol as well. In this group of patients, L-carnitine not only decreased plasma triglyceride levels but also increased HDL levels, making patients more resistant to developing atherosclerosis.

For those patients with normal levels of HDL and high levels of triglycerides, there was no triglyceride lowering associated with L-carnitine supplementation. So it would appear that the use of L-carnitine in dialysis patients with hypertriglyceridemia also may benefit those with low HDL levels. This relationship was also verified in an earlier study, when fifty-one chronic hemodialysis patients with hypertriglyceridemia were given 2.4 grams of L-carnitine for thirty days. Serum triglyceride concentrations decreased significantly while total serum cholesterol did not change.[52] However, HDL cholesterol increased significantly, suggesting that administering L-carnitine to dialysis patients with high triglycerides and low HDLs can help correct these lipid abnormalities. One could then speculate upon a risk reduction for atherosclerosis in this subpopulation of renal patients. I suggest that these findings also may be applied to the general population.

In one Italian study of twenty-six patients with high cholesterol and triglycerides, 3 grams of oral carnitine per day showed a significant reduction in plasma lipids.[53] In their study, not only did carnitine reduce serum triglycerides and total serum cholesterol, it increased blood levels of HDL as well. The researchers speculated that carnitine deficiency would result in faulty fatty acid utilization through the reduction of beta-oxidation, resulting in the increased synthesis of cholesterol acids and triglycerides. Remember, the mechanism of action of L-carnitine is in the transport of free fatty acids through the intramitochondrial membrane. When carnitine levels fall in the blood, the impaired oxidation of fatty acids results in abnormal lipid levels. Sometimes the use of carnitine can have some dramatic effects in individual case studies.

The Johns Hopkins Medical Journal reported the effect of carnitine on serum HDL in two patients.[54] One gram of L-carnitine administered over a period of fifteen weeks had shown tremendous increase in HDL cholesterol, as much as 63 percent and 94 percent, respectively. There also was a decrease in total triglycerides by about 25 percent during the period of carnitine treatment. The researchers speculated that carnitine was activating an enzyme called *lipoprotein lipase*, which lowers serum triglycerides while raising HDL. Since low levels of HDL are a serious risk factor for coronary disease, raising the HDL to respectable levels definitely will reduce your cardiac risk. Research shows that the ratio of LDL to HDL is a better predictor for heart attack than total cholesterol, LDL, or HDL alone. A ratio of 5:1 or greater (LDL to HDL) was associated with a much higher risk for heart attack than a ratio below five. L-carnitine is one supplement that certainly should be considered for raising HDL levels. Carnitine also has cardioprotective properties, and another area where carnitine preserves myocardial tissue is its protection against drug toxicity.

ADRIAMYCIN TOXICITY

Carnitine has been shown to protect against the damaging effects on the heart produced by the chemotherapeutic drug called *Adriamycin*, which is used in the treatment of many cancers and lymphomas. The cardiac damage induced by *anthracycline antibiotics, daunorubicin,* and *doxorubicin,* is very real. I have seen patients with severe cardiac complications due to these agents, including heart failure, and even death. These chemotherapy agents not only kill rapidly proliferative cancer cells, they're also toxic to normal heart cells. Disruption of basement membranes and an increase of free fatty acids and long-chain toxic fatty acid metabolites all can injure the myocardial cells. Research has shown that L-carnitine may have the ability to prevent the toxic complications of these drugs.[55,56,57]

SUMMARY OF CARDIOVASCULAR INTERACTIONS

In conclusion, the cardiovascular data in both human and animal studies support the use of carnitine supplementation in the prevention and treatment of a wide variety of cardiovascular diseases. Carnitine by itself, or in combination with magnesium and CoQ10, has been a terrific nutritional support in my practice of cardiology. Improvements have been seen in exercise tolerance; reduction in angina, antiarrhythmic and hypolipidemic actions; reduction in the use of prescribed drugs, particularly nitroglycerin; cardiac function; quality of life; and even in survival rates. Although additional studies will help to establish L-carnitine as a cardioprotective agent in the treatment of cardiovascular diseases, all the research thus far has demonstrated neither toxicity nor detrimental effects during L-carnitine administration. Like coenzyme Q10, carnitine appears to be safe and efficacious.

The combination of carnitine and coenzyme Q10 offers tremendous hope as an adjunct to conventional medicine, which can help ease human suffering and improve survival. In the next section, we will investigate the interaction of these "twin pillars of healing."

CARNITINE AND COENZYME Q10: ANTIAGING NUTRIENTS FOR HEALTH AND LONGEVITY

Earlier, I referred to carnitine and coenzyme Q10 as the "twin pillars of healing." In this section I want to briefly describe my reasons for using this descriptive phrase.

First of all, let's look at how these nutrients function in the body, that is, their biochemical mechanism of action. The primary role of carnitine is to facilitate the oxidation of fatty acids by transporting them into the mitochondrial matrix. Fatty acids (derived from fats) cannot by themselves traverse mitochondria; they need a specialized transport mechanism. This is where carnitine comes in (see Figure 1). By conjugating, or binding, itself to a fatty acid molecule, carnitine can transport the fatty acid to the inner mitochondrial membrane. The carnitine molecule then goes back and transports another fatty acid molecule, and so on. This process is called the "carnitine shuttle."

Once in the mitochondria, the fatty acids are first activated (by conjugation with coenzyme A) and then broken down for further processing. (A *coenzyme*, as its name suggests, is an essential component of an enzyme system, and coenzyme A is necessary for many enzyme systems in our body to function.) The final step is the production of the vital biological energy ATP, via the electron transport chain. Think of mitochondria as a furnace and carnitine as a delivery service. Carnitine delivers the fuel necessary to keep the fire going constantly. This illustrates the importance of carnitine in energy production.

Another function of carnitine is to prevent the accumulation of excess free and bound fatty acids in the mitochondria, which can be harmful to the cellular and intracellular membranes. Carnitine conjugates with these fatty acids and transports them out of the mitochondria. This activity confers upon carnitine a vital role as a physiologic modulator of mitochondrial function, as it regulates the ratio of two key compounds: acetyl-coenzyme A to coenzyme A. When this ratio is decreased—by transporting the acetyl group out of the mitochondria and thus freeing up coenzyme A—glucose oxidation is enhanced by stimulation of a key enzyme system, called *pyruvate dehydrogenase complex.*

The primary function of coenzyme Q10 is energy production. Every cell in our body needs energy to survive and to function properly. What we eat provides the fuel to produce this energy. The conversion process takes place in the mitochondria, via the electron transport chain. This highly organized structure is composed of a series of enzyme systems. Coenzyme Q10, as the name suggests, has a critical function in shuttling electrons between these enzyme systems. It is through this process that the biological energy called ATP is generated. Coenzyme Q10 literally provides the spark to run the mitochondrial energy production necessary for our body's functions. If our supply of coenzyme Q10 becomes limited, so will our energy supply. There is a direct connection between the two.

While all cells, tissues, and organs need energy, the demand is much higher for some. Your heart is a very good example. The heart has one of the highest concentrations of CoQ10 and there must be a reason: Because our heart needs a constant supply of a high amount of energy for efficient operation, its function will be compromised if the availability of Coenzyme Q10 is inadequate.

In addition to its important role in energy production, coenzyme Q10 is an excellent antioxidant. Because of its wide distribution in all cellular membranes—blood as well as serum lipoproteins—CoQ10 can efficiently protect all these components from oxidant stress.

Having learned the important roles played by both carnitine and coenzyme Q10 at the molecular and functional levels, you now can appreciate the importance of these nutrients in maintaining our health. Both of them are essential for energy production, and they work as a team. One delivers the fuel and the other helps burn it! If either one fails, the whole system fails. There is no backup. This is why we call carnitine and coenzyme Q10 the "twin pillars of healing," because of the crucial nature of their role in our health. Let me give you a few examples of their application when these nutrients are used together.

Bertelli and coworkers at the University of Milan in Italy have demonstrated the protective and synergistic effects of carnitine and coenzyme Q10 on several conditions, such as ischemia and reperfusion injury of the heart; fatty infiltration of the liver induced by alcohol; and hyperbaric oxygen toxicity in experimental animals.[58,59,60] The synergy between carnitine and CoQ10 is explained on the basis of these nutrients' biochemical and metabolic complementary roles.[61] Based on a review of published research, McCarty recommends a combination of carnitine and CoQ10 (among other nutrients) for patients with congestive heart failure.[62]

Mitochondrial cytopathies (also known as myopathies) are a cluster of disorders related to mitochondrial dysfunction. One direct consequence of these disorders is impaired energy production. Depending upon where the molecular defect occurs in the electron transport chain, coenzyme Q10 alone, or in combination with carnitine, has been found to be beneficial in these disorders. In fact, there is a wealth of literature on their therapeutic use. For instance, Wada and coworkers recently reported a case in which they successfully treated a patient with a combination of carnitine and coenzyme Q10.[63]

It is important to recognize that you do not have to have an abnormal medical condition to benefit from carnitine and CoQ10 supplementation. Normal, healthy individuals also can derive benefit from these nutrients. *The objective here is to minimize your risk for future health problems.* This strategy is known as *prevention*, for you must be one step ahead of the game when it comes to your health. There are other situations where a combination of these nutrients could be very helpful, such as athletics and activities involving strenuous muscular work. Carnitine and coenzyme Q10 together can help in several ways. First and foremost, they help meet the greater demand for energy. In addition, they can counter the increase in oxidant stress associated with physical exertion. Reducing the accumulation of harmful metabolites such as lactate is another important function that can help reduce muscular fatigue.

What are the preferred forms of carnitine and coenzyme Q10, and how much should we take as nutritional supplements? There are a number of forms (derivatives) of carnitine, which are discussed in the next section. As for coenzyme Q10, the forms available vary, using pure coenzyme Q10 powder. *It is important to note that not all forms are created equal in terms of performance.*

L-CARNITINE FUMARATE

Carnitine in the free (base) form is very hygroscopic, that is, it draws moisture and is unstable; therefore, this free form is not suitable for making tablets or capsules. This has led to research on ways to deliver stable forms of L-carnitine possessing desirable properties and good handling characteristics. Several forms have been synthesized; among them are *fumarate, tartrate, citrate,* and *lactate.*

To render L-carnitine less hygroscopic and more stable at ambient conditions, Sigma-tau S.p.A. has developed and patented a method to produce *L-Carnitine Fumarate* (Sigma-tau U.S. patent #4,602,039), which has demonstrated the best overall profile for good handling characteristics: low hydroscopicity, stability, and bioavailability. This increased bioavailability may be attributable to the very fine particle size of the L-Carnitine Fumarate, which translates into an increased surface area overall so that dissolution can occur more rapidly once the tablet disintegrates in the gut. This is especially important for its application as a cardiac supplement, its ability to increase oxygen transport, and to "super-charge" the efficacy of coenzyme Q10 (see Figure 3).

These are the highlights of L-Carnitine Fumarate:

1. Combining L-carnitine and fumarate has a double effect in energy production. The first is direct, as L-carnitine shuttles free fatty acids into the mitochondria to improve ATP generation during the Krebs energy cycle. Second, fumaric acid, as a naturally occurring substance in our body, takes part in the Krebs cycle by boosting energy production. It also exerts a free radical scavenger action through its antioxidant properties.

2. For L-Carnitine Fumarate, both L-carnitine and fumaric acid are produced using an entirely synthetic process. No biotechnology or genetically modified (GM) organisms are involved. Consequently, there are no concerns about microbiological waste residue in finished goods or about waste treatment.

3. L-Carnitine Fumarate is highly stable and delivers superior handling and formulation characteristics.

4. Recently released research performed at George Washington University Medical Center indicates that L-Carnitine Fumarate delivers a sparing effect in ischemic heart disease.

Figure 3 The Metabolism of L-Carnitine Fumarate

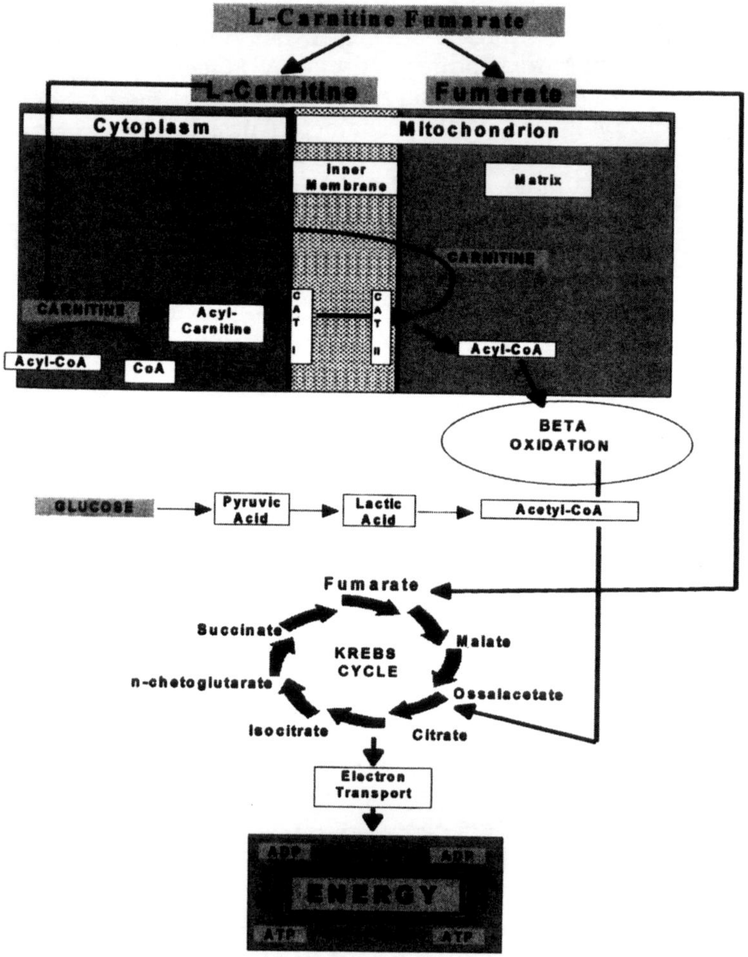

HYDROSOLUBLE COENZYME Q10

Coenzyme Q10 is insoluble in water and very poorly soluble
in fats. As you might expect, this can affect its absorption.
There is a simple laboratory test, called *the dissolution test,*

which can predict bioavailability in human subjects. In this test, tablets and capsules made with the coenzyme Q10 powder failed the test completely! This provided the impetus for research on a more bioavailable form of CoQ10. A new *hydrosoluble* form was developed recently (covered by a patent pending process) using a unique process called Biosolv.

The bioavailability-enhancing effect of the Biosolv process is accomplished in two ways: a dramatic reduction in the particle size of the nutrient and an increase in the hydrophilicity of the nutrient (with a corresponding decrease in its hydrophobicity). This is achieved using special processing techniques and the incorporation of a proprietary blend of ingredients. In order to facilitate improved absorption, particle sizes of the nutrients must be in the submicron range. The formulation also must contain ingredients that enhance the surface activity of the active components. The Biosolv process accomplishes both of these objectives, with the result of enhanced absorption and improved bioavailability.

When tested in the laboratory, Biosolv process showed an amazing 100 percent dissolution, which was predictive of excellent bioavailability in human subjects. A human study then was carried out to compare the new hydrosoluble coenzyme Q10 with other products on the market. The results confirmed the superiority of the hydrosoluble product.[64] Maintaining proper blood levels of CoQ10 is very important, and this hydrosoluble form will enable the nutrient to more quickly reach much higher levels in the blood.

Single entity products are widely available in many drug stores and health food stores. Because of the recognition of the importance of combining carnitine and coenzyme Q10 in human health and the science confirming it, products based on these two important nutrients are now readily available, such as Carni-Q-Gel™ and Q-Carni™ softgels, to name just two. Interestingly, a patent was issued for this novel combination of L-carnitine and CoQ10 in 1986 (Sigma-tau, U.S. patent #4,599,232). The products containing the hydrosoluble form of CoQ10 and L-Carnitine Fumarate (Sigma-tau) are manufactured under a license issued by the holder of this patent.

DOSAGE RECOMMENDATIONS, DRUG INTERACTIONS, AND ADVERSE REACTIONS

Because L-carnitine, like coenzyme Q10, is a substance made by the body, its supplemental administration, as expected, causes few (if any) side effects. I've been using L-carnitine for the last several years and have yet to see any side effects, other than some fleeting gastrointestinal (GI) complaints. Should these side effects occur, I usually tell my patients to take a lower dosage or perhaps take their dose with a small amount of food. Although carnitine is absorbed more efficiently on an empty stomach, improved delivery systems are being developed by manufacturers, especially softgel combinations that use the fumarate derivative of carnitine. These preparations offer more bioavailability so they can be taken with food, and any GI reactions will be limited.

I usually recommend doses of 250 to 500 mg of L-Carnitine Fumarate (Sigma-tau) three to four times daily. It's often best to start at the lower end of the dose range and then double or triple the dose to get the desired therapeutic effect. Remember that L-carnitine, coenzyme Q10, and other nutrients may require individual dose adjustments; there's no automatic dose of these agents that is best for everyone. L-carnitine, like many supplements, may require dosage adjustments to obtain optimum therapeutic blood levels and symptom relief.

For example, for coenzyme Q10 to be effective in compromised cardiac patients, its level in the blood frequently needs to be greater than five or six times the normal blood level. Many people will not realize a therapeutic effect with coenzyme Q10, even if their blood level is at two or three times above normal. The same may be true for L-carnitine supplementation. In some of my patients, 500 to 1,500 mg of L-carnitine, although a suitable dose, may not be an effective therapeutic dose. Occasionally, doses need to be increased to 3 or 4 grams daily.

Although the optimum dosage of L-carnitine for the management of cardiovascular disorders has yet to be established, most clinical cardiologists would agree that adjusting the dose while at the same time tracking subjective and objective information is the best way to determine the optimum dose for any individual. But we have to ask ourselves, Can L-carnitine be toxic in large dosages?

In my experience, and after reviewing the medical literature, I can attest that L-carnitine is completely safe, even at high doses. According to one author, carnitine is probably one of the safest nutritional supports on earth![65]

However, when considering daily doses, it's possible that the compromised renal patient may require lower doses. In one small study using 3 grams of L-carnitine a day, a paradoxical effect on triglyceride levels and an increase in blood clotting was observed in some patients on hemodialysis,[66] although other clinical research has failed to support this one finding. If you look at the data from the overall medical literature, you will find that L-carnitine is considered to be extremely safe.

OTHER INTERACTIONS

As I discussed in the beginning of this Good Health Guide, there appears to be a synergistic relationship between coenzyme Q10 and carnitine, making them, in my opinion, the best "one-two punch" there is for treating angina, heart failure, arrhythmia, and many other aspects of cardiovascular disease. This synergy also has been documented in the medical literature, particularly in the setting of ischemia.[67] I've also seen a potentiating effect among coenzyme Q10, L-carnitine, and pantetheine in significantly raising HDL, even in my most refractory cardiac patients—the ones with low HDL and coronary artery disease. The synergism between carnitine and pantetheine has been validated in the literature, as well.[68]

ADVERSE DRUG INTERACTIONS

There have been some drug interactions related to L-carnitine. For example, anticonvulsant drugs, including *phenobarbital, phenytoin*

(Dilantin®), and *carbamazepine* (Tegretol®), have had a significant lowering effect on serum L-carnitine levels.[69] Similarly, in children, *pivampicillin* (an antibiotic) has been shown to have a negative effect on carnitine metabolism.[70] Of course, we already discussed the relationship of L-carnitine and Adriamycin toxicity.

SUMMARY

Over the past two decades, carnitine has been shown to be a critical component of energy metabolism, and its role as an effective nutrient can no longer be ignored. The many uses of carnitine go far beyond therapeutic and preventive regimens. Carnitine functions as an antioxidant, helps to generate ATP, and serves to transport fats into the mitochondria where beta-oxidation occurs. Its use in a number of cardiovascular diseases and situations has been explored and found to be positive.

Health conditions that may benefit from carnitine supplementation are literally too numerous to count. The fact that there are multiple patents on carnitine for a wide number of medical situations testifies to its clinical usefulness. As one prominent cardiologist has stated, "One challenge for the future is to find safer and more effective pharmacological therapies, and the data reviewed suggest that carnitine warrants further attention."[71] Carnitine is completely safe, with no known toxic effects. It is one nutrient that today's cardiologists should strongly consider in their battle against cardiovascular disease.

REFERENCES

1. Neely, J. R., and H. A. Morgan. "Relationships Between Carbo-hydrate Metabolism and Energy Balance of the Heart Muscle." *Annual Review of Physiology* 36 (1974): 413–59.

2. Miquel, J. "Theoretical and Experimental Support for an 'Oxygen Radical-Mitochondrial Injury' Hypothesis of Cell Aging," in *Free Radicals, Aging, and Degenerative Diseases,* edited by J. E. Johnson, R. Walford, D. Harman, and J. Miquel, 51–55. New York: Aland R. Liss, 1986.

3. Smith, J. B., C. M. Ingerman, and M. J. Silver. "Malondialde-hyde Formation as an Indicator of Prostaglandin Production by Human Platelets." *Journal of Laboratory and Clinical Medicine* 88 (1976): 167–72.

4. Babior, M. B. "Oxygen Dependent Microbial Killing by Phago-cytes." *New England Journal of Medicine* 298, no. 12 (1978): 659–68.

5. Kelly, G. S. "L-Carnitine: Therapeutic Applications of a Conditionally Essential Amino Acid." *Alternative Medicine Review* 3, no. 5 (1998): 345–60.

6. Council on Foods and Nutrition. "Zen Macrobiotic Diets." *Journal of the American Medical Association* 218, no. 3 (1971): 397.

7. Delanghe, J., et al. "Normal Reference Values for Creatine, Creatinine, and Carnitine Are Lower in Vegetarians." *Clinical Chemistry* 35, no. 8 (1989): 1802–3.

8. Dwyer, J. T., et al. "Risk of Nutritional Rickets Among Vegetarian Children." *American Journal of Diseases in Children* 133, no. 2 (1979): 134–40.

9. Cederblad, G., and S. Lindstedt. "Metabolism of Labeled Carnitine in the Rat." *Archives of Biochemistry and Biophysics* 175 (1976): 173–82.

10. Yeh, T. "Antiketonemic and Antiketogenic Actions of Carnitine *in Vivo* and *in Vitro* in Rats." *Journal of Nutrition* 111 (1981): 831–40.

11. Opie, L. H. "Role of Carnitine in Fatty Acid Metabolism of Normal and Ischemic Myocardium." *American Heart Journal* 97 (1979): 375–88.

12. Bahl, J. J., and R. Bressler. "The Pharmacology of Carnitine." *Annual Review of Pharmacology and Toxicology* 27 (1987): 257–77.

13. Rebouche, C., and D. Paulson. "Carnitine Metabolism and Function in Humans." *Annual Review of Nutrition* 6 (1986): 41–66.

14. Brevetti, G., M. Chiariello, G. Ferulano, et al. "Increases in Walking Distance in Patients with Peripheral Vascular Disease Treated with L-Carnitine: A Double-blind, Cross-over Study." *Circulation* 77 (1988): 767–73.

15. Ohtsuka, Y., and O. Griffith. "L-Carnitine Protection in Ammonia Intoxication." *Biochemical Pharmacology* 41 (1991): 1957–61.

16. Arduini, A. "Carnitine and Its Acyl Esters as Secondary Antioxidants?" *American Heart Journal* 123 (1992): 1726–27.

17. Uematsu, T., T. Itaya, M. Nishimoto, et al. "Pharmacokinetics and Safety of L-Carnitine-infused IV in Healthy Subjects." *European Journal of Clinical Pharmacology* 34 (1988): 213–16.

18. Harper, P., C. E. Elwin, and G. Cederblad. "Pharmacokinetics of Intravenous and Oral Bolus Doses of L-Carnitine in Healthy Subjects." *European Journal of Clinical Pharmacology* 35 (1988): 555–62.

19. Bach, A. C., H. Schirardin, M. O. Sihr, and D. Storck. "Free and Total Carnitine in Human Serum After Oral Ingestion of L-Carnitine." *Diabetes and Metabolism* 9 (1983): 121–24.

20. Chopra, R., R. Goldman, S. Sinatra, et al. "Relative Bioavailability of Coenzyme Q10 Formulations in Human Subjects." *International Journal for Vitamin and Nutrition Research* 68, no. 2 (1998): 109–13.

21. Laplante, A., et al. "Effects and Metabolism of Fumarate in Reperfused Rat Heart: A 13C Mass Isotopomer Study." *American Journal of Physiology* 272 (1997): 74–82.

22. Pepine, C. J. "The Therapeutic Potential of Carnitine in Cardiovascular Disorders." *Clinical Therapeutics* 13, no. 1 (1991): 2–21.
23. Waber, L., D. Valle, C. Neill, et al. "Carnitine Deficiency Presenting as Familial Cardiomyopathy: A Treatable Defect in Carnitine Transport." *Journal of Pediatrics* 101 (1982): 700–705.
24. Neely, J. R., and H. A. Morgan. "Relationships Between Carbohydrate Metabolism and Energy Balance of Heart Muscle." *Annual Review of Physiology* 36 (1974): 413–59.
25. Littarru, G. P., L. Ho, and K. Folkers. "Deficiency of Coenzyme Q10 in Human Heart Disease, Part I." *International Journal for Vitamin and Nutrition Research* 42, no. 2 (1972): 291; "Deficiency of Coenzyme Q10 in Human Heart Disease, Part II." *International Journal for Vitamin and Nutrition Research* 42, no. 3 (1972): 413.
26. Narin, F., N. Narin, H. Andac, et al. "Carnitine Levels in Patients with Chronic Rheumatic Heart Disease." *Clinical Biochemistry* 30, no. 8 (1997): 643–45.
27. Opie, L. H. "Role of Carnitine in Fatty Acid Metabolism of Normal and Ischemic Myocardium." *American Heart Journal* 97 (1979): 373–78.
28. Goa, K. L., and R. N. Brogden. "L-Carnitine: A Preliminary Review of Its Pharmacokinetics, and Its Therapeutic Use in Ischemic Cardiac Disease and Primary and Secondary Carnitine Deficiencies in Relationship to Its Role in Fatty Acid Metabolism." *Drugs* 34 (1987): 1–24.
29. Silverman, N. A., G. Schmitt, M. Vishwanath, et al. "Effect of Carnitine on Myocardial Function and Metabolism Following Global Ischemia." *Annals of Thoracic Surgery* 40 (1985): 20–25.
30. Pepine, C. J. "The Therapeutic Potential of Carnitine in Cardiovascular Disorders." *Clinical Therapeutics* 13 (1991): 2–21.
31. Kamikawa, T., Y. Suzuki, A. Kobayashi, et al. "Effects of L-Carnitine on Exercise Tolerance in Patients with Stable Angina Pectoris." *Japanese Heart Journal* 25, no. 4 (1984): 587–96.
32. Cacciatore, L., R. Cerio, M. Ciarimboli, M. Cocozza, et al. "The Therapeutic Effect of L-Carnitine in Patients with Exercise-induced Stable Angina: A Controlled Study." *Drugs Under Experimental and Clinical Research* XVII, no. 4 (1991): 225–335.
33. Thomsen, J. H., A. L. Shug, U. Y. Viscente, et al. "Improved Pacing Tolerance of the Ischemic Human Myocardium After

Administration of Carnitine." *The American Journal of Cardiology* 43 (1979): 300–6.

34. Suzuki, Y., Y. Masumura, A. Kobayashi, et al. "Myocardial Carnitine Deficiency in Chronic Heart Failure." *The Lancet* 1, no. 8263 (1982): 116.

35. Spagnoli, L. G., M. Corsi, S. Villaschi, et al. "Myocardial Carnitine Deficiency in Acute Myocardial Infarction." *The Lancet* 1 (1982): 165.

36. Singh, R. B., M. A. Niaz, P. Agarwal, et al. "A Randomized, Double-blind, Placebo-controlled Trial of L-Carnitine in Suspected Acute Myocardial Infarction." *Postgraduate Medicine* 72 (1996): 45–50.

37. Iliceto, S., D. Scrutinio, P. Bruzzi, et al. "Effects of L-Carnitine Administration on Left Ventricular Remodeling After Acute Anterior Myocardial Infarction: The L-Carnitine Ecocardiografia Digitalizzata Infarto Miocardioco (CEDIM) Trial." *Journal of the American College of Cardiology* 26, no. 2 (1995): 380–87.

38. Davini, P., A. Bigalli, F. Lamanna, and A. Boem. "Controlled Study on L-Carnitine Therapeutic Efficacy in Post-infarction." *Drugs Under Experimental and Clinical Research* 18 (1992): 355–65.

39. Singh, R. B., M. A. Niaz, P. Agarwal, et al. "A Randomized, Double-blind, Placebo-controlled Trial of L-Carnitine in Suspected Acute Myocardial Infarction." *Postgraduate Medical Journal* 72 (1996): 45–50.

40. Iliceto, S., D. Scrutinio, P. Bruzzi, et al. "Effects of L-Carnitine Administration on Left Ventricular Remodeling After Acute Anterior Myocardial Infarction: The L-Carnitine Ecocardiografia Digitalizzata Infarto Miocardioco (CEDIM) Trial." *Journal of the American College of Cardiology* 26, no. 2 (1995): 380–87.

41. Kobayashi, A., M. Yoshinori, and N. Yamazaki. "L-Carnitine Treatment for Congestive Heart Failure: Experimental and Clinical Study." *Japanese Circulation Journal* 56 (1992): 86–94.

42. Bashore, T. M., D. J. Magorien, J. Letterio, et al. "Histologic and Biochemical Correlates of Left Ventricular Chamber Dynamics in Man." *Journal of Molecular and Cell Cardiology* 9 (1987): 734.

43. Hiatt, W. R., D. Nawaz, E. P. Brass. "Carnitine Metabolism During Exercise in Patients with Peripheral Arterial Disease." *Journal of Applied Physiology* 62 (1987): 2383–87.

44. Brevetti, G., M. Chiariello, G. Ferulano, et al. "Increases in Walking Distance in Patients with L-Carnitine: A Double-blind, Cross-over Study." *Circulation* 77 (1988): 767–73.
45. Oliver, M. F., V. A. Kurien, and T. W. Greenwood. "Relation Between Serum Free Fatty Acids and Arrhythmias and Death After Acute Myocardial Infarction." *The Lancet* 1 (1968): 710.
46. Suzuki, Y., T. Kamikawa, and N. Yamazaki. "Effects of L-Carnitine on Ventricular Arrhythmias in Dogs with Acute Myocardial Ischemia and a Supplement of Excess Free Fatty Acids." *Japanese Circulation Journal* 45 (1981): 552–59.
47. Rizzon, P., G. Biasco, M. Di Biase, et al. "High Doses of L-Carnitine in Acute Myocardial Infarction: Metabolic and Anti-arrhythmic Effects." *European Heart Journal* 10 (1989): 502–8.
48. Ghidini, O., M. Azzurro, G. Vita, and G. Sartori. "Evaluation of the Therapeutic Efficacy of L-Carnitine in Congestive Heart Failure." *International Journal of Clinical Pharmacology and Therapeutic Toxicology* 26, no. 4 (1988): 217–20.
49. Suzuki, Y., M. Narita, and N. Yamazaki. "Effects of L-Carnitine on Arrhythmias During Hemodialysis." *Japanese Heart Journal* 23 (1982): 349–59.
50. Borum, P. R., and E. M. Taggart. "Carnitine Nutriture of Dialysis Patients." *Journal of the American Dietetic Association* 86, no. 5 (1986): 644–47.
51. Vacha, G., G. Giorcelli, N. Siliprandi, and M. Corsi. "Favorable Effects of L-Carnitine Treatment on Hypertriglyceridemia in Hemodialysis Patients: Decisive Role of Low Levels of High-density Lipoprotein-cholesterol." *American Journal of Clinical Nutrition* 38 (1983): 532.
52. Lacour, B., J. Chanard, M. Hauet, et al. "Carnitine Improves Lipid Anomalies in Hemodialysis Patients." *The Lancet* 2, no. 8198 (1980): 763–64.
53. Pola, P., L. Savi, M. Grilli, et al. "Carnitine in the Therapy of Dyslipidemic Patients." *Current Therapeutic Research* 27, no. 2 (1980): 208–16.
54. Rossi, C., and N. Silirandi. "Effect of Carnitine on Serum HDL-Cholesterol: Report of Two Cases." *The Johns Hopkins Medical Journal* 150, no. 2 (1982): 51–54.
55. Neri, B., T. Comparini, A. Miliani, et al. "Protective Effects of L-Carnitine (Carnitine) on Acute Adriamycin and Daunomycin

Cardiotoxicity in Cancer Patients." *Clinical Trials Journal* 20 (1983): 98–103.

56. De Leonardis, V., B. Neri, S. Bacalli, and P. Cinelli. "Reduction of Cardiac Toxicity of Anthracyclines by L-Carnitine: Preliminary Overview of Clinical Data." *International Journal of Clinical Pharmacology Research* 5 (1985): 137–42.

57. Chavez, G. A., I. M. Hernandez, C. F. Ollarve, et al. "Myocardial Protection by L-Carnitine in Children Treated with Adriamycin." *Review of Latin American Cardiology Euroamerican* 18 (1997): 208–14.

58. Bertelli, A., A. A. Bertelli, L. Giovannini, and P. Spaggiari. "Protective Synergic Effect of Coenzyme Q10 and Carnitine on Hyperbaric Oxygen Toxicity." *International Journal of Tissue Reactions* 12 (1990): 193–96.

59. Bertelli, A., F. Ronca, G. Ronca, L. Palmieri, and R. Zucchi. "L-Carnitine and Coenzyme Q10 Protective Action Against Ischemia and Reperfusion of Working Rat Heart." *Drugs Under Experimental and Clinical Research* 18 (1992): 431–36.

60. Bertelli, A., A. Cerrati, L. Giovannini, M. Mian, P. Spaggiari, and A. A. Bertelli. "Protective Action of L-carnitine and Coenzyme Q10 Against Hepatic Triglyceride Infiltration Induced by Hyperbaric Oxygen and Ethanol." *Drugs Under Experimental and Clinical Research* 19 (1993): 65–68.

61. Bertelli, A., and G. Ronca. "Carnitine and Coenzyme Q10: Biochemical Properties and Functions, Synergism, and Complementary Action." *International Journal of Tissue Reactions* 12 (1990): 183–86.

62. McCarty, M. F. "Fish Oil and Other Nutritional Adjuvants for Treatment of Congestive Heart Failure." *Medical Hypotheses* 46 (1996): 400–406.

63. Wada, H., H. Nishio, S. Nagaki, H. Yanagawa, A. Imamura, S. Yokoyama, T. Sano, M. Woo, M. Matsuo, H. Itoh, and H. Nakamura. "Benign Infantile Mitochondrial Myopathy Caused by Reversible Cytochrome C Oxidase Deficiency." *No To Hattatsu* 28 (1996): 443–47.

64. Chopra, R. K., R. Goldman, S. T. Sinatra, and H. N. Bhagavan. "Relative Bioavailability of Coenzyme Q10 Formulations in Human Subjects." *International Journal of Vitamin and Nutrition Research* 68 (1998): 109–13.

65. Leibovitz, B. E. *L-Carnitine: The Energy Nutrient* (Keats Good Health Guide). Los Angeles: Keats Publishing, 1998.

66. Weschler, A., et al. "High Dose of L-Carnitine Increases Platelet Aggregation and Plasma Triglyceride Levels in Uremic Patients on Hemodialysis." *Nephron* 38 (1984): 120–24.

67. Bertelli, A., et al. "L-Carnitine and Coenzyme Q10 Protective Action Against Ischaemia and Reperfusion of Working Rat Heart." *Drugs Under Experimental Clinical Research* 18 (1992): 431–36.

68. Gleeson, J. M., et al. "Effect of Carnitine and Pantetheine on the Metabolic Abnormalities of Acquired Total Lipodystrophy." *Current Therapeutic Research* 41 (1987): 83–88.

69. Hug, G., C. A. McGraw, S. R. Bates, and E. A. Landrigan. "Reduction of Serum Carnitine Concentrations During Anticonvulsant Therapy with Phenobarbital, Valproic Acid, Phenytoin, and Carbamazepine in Children." *Journal of Pediatrics* 119 (1991): 799–802.

70. Melegh, B., M. Pap, D. Molnar, et al. "Carnitine Administration Ameliorates the Changes in Energy Metabolism Caused by Short-term Pivampicillin Medication." *European Journal of Pediatrics* 156 (1997): 795–99.

71. Pepine, C. J. "The Therapeutic Potential of Carnitine in Cardiovascular Disorders." *Clinical Therapeutics* 13, no. 1 (1991): 2–21.